ASSEMBLY AT WESTMINSTER

The Humble

ADVICE
Of the

ASSEMBLY
OF

DIVINES,

Now by Authority of *Parliament*
sitting at WESTMINSTER,

Concerning
A Confeßion of Faith :

With the QUOTATIONS and TEXTS of
SCRIPTURE annexed.

Presented by them lately to both Houses of Parliament.

Printed at LONDON;
AND
Re-printed at EDINBURGH by *Evan Tyler*, Printer to
the Kings moſt Excellent Majeſtie. 1647.

ASSEMBLY AT WESTMINSTER

Reformed Theology in the Making

JOHN H. LEITH

JOHN KNOX PRESS
Atlanta

Library of Congress Cataloging in Publication Data

Leith, John H
  Assembly at Westminster.

  Includes bibliographical references.
  1. Westminster confession of faith. 2. Westminster
Assembly of Divines. I. Title.
BX9183.L44   238'.5'1   72–11162
ISBN 0–8042–0885–9

To

WILLIAM HARTNETTE LEITH
1875–1930
Ruling Elder
Superintendent of the Sunday School
and
LUCY HADDON LEITH
1887–1973
President of the Woman's Auxiliary

Parents who began my attendance, if not participation,
in church services when I was a few weeks of age
and who are responsible for my earliest memories
being memories of life in the church.

PREFACE

This study was undertaken to document the historical and human character of the Westminster Confession. Only when the historical character of the Confession is freely acknowledged can it be a guide for Christian thinking and preaching today.

It is hoped that this study will illuminate the nature of the theological enterprise by examining an important example of it. Theology is understood in this study as dialogue, that is, as the Christian community's effort to articulate its faith under the norm of the Christian revelation and in the context of a particular time and place. As such, theology is an endless task.

It is also hoped that this study will be useful to ruling elders and to church members who affirm the Confession as their authoritative statement of faith. Without a historical understanding of the Confession this is a difficult affirmation, but with an awareness of the historical character of the Confession and of the theological enterprise generally, this can be a meaningful act of faith and churchmanship.

The writer is indebted to many teachers and friends, and to the nurture and sustenance of a church which has had the Westminster Confession as its subordinate standard. Gratitude must be expressed for the good offices of Union Theological Seminary in Virginia and for its excellent library. A Folger Shakespeare Library fellowship in 1965 made possible research at that remarkable institution. Financial resources for research were also provided by the Advanced Religious Studies Foundation of Texas and by Union Theological Seminary in Virginia. The resources of the McAlpin Collection of Union Theological Seminary in New York were also made available to me. My colleague John Newton Thomas read the manuscript and made helpful suggestions.

John H. Leith
Union Theological Seminary in Virginia
December 1972

Contents

INTRODUCTION

The study of the Westminster Confession and Catechisms is justified, even in an age of nuclear power and politics and of theological openness to the future, on at least four grounds. First of all, the Confession and Catechisms have been the basic creedal documents of English-speaking Presbyterians for more than three centuries. They have likewise exercised significant influence in Congregational and Baptist traditions. Secondly, the Confession and the Catechisms bring to a climax in a grand and monumental way one of the very great theological periods in the history of the Christian church. Thirdly, the Confession's place in the history of Christian doctrine is such that a grasp of its significance is important in understanding the contemporary theological situation. Finally, the Confession and the Catechisms illustrate both the achievements and the perils of the theological enterprise in general.

The Westminster Assembly and its work have been slighted by the historians of thought and also by church historians.[1] Reasons for the neglect are apparent. The Assembly was the offspring of a political movement that failed. It was primarily theological, not philosophical, and it came at the end of an age. It was not creative of the modern world, though it may be argued that it gave strength and character to many who did participate significantly in the modern world. Cultural aversions to the thought and style of the Puritans likewise influenced later historians. The overlooking or the minimizing of the Westminster Assembly can be understood, but the Assembly need not be accepted at face value.

For three hundred years the work of the Westminster Assembly was the primary theological rubric of English-speaking Presbyterians. It was likewise influential with their theological kinsmen in Congregational and Baptist churches. The Westminster Confession was adopted with a few modifications as the Savoy Declaration of the English Congregational churches. It was adopted by the Congregational Synod of Cambridge, Massachusetts, in 1648, and with the Savoy modification, by the Synod of Boston in 1680, and by the Congregational churches of Connecticut at the Synod of Saybrook in 1708.[2] It was adopted with modification by the London Baptists in 1677 and in America as the Baptist Confession of 1742 (Philadelphia).[3] Certainly the number of children who received their religious instruction from the Shorter Catechism must be estimated in the millions. The sheer number of persons who have been influenced by the Confession and Catechisms of the Westminster Assembly merits far greater attention for the Assembly than it has received from scholars.

The Westminster Confession was one of the final documents of the great period of theological activity that began on October 31, 1517, with Luther's ninety-five theses. The theological achievement of the Reformers during the first half of the sixteenth century is sometimes contrasted with the theological work among Protestants after Calvin's death in 1564. There is no question that the first period is characterized by renewal, by the expectancy and even ecstasy of new insight and discovery, and that the second period is characterized by careful definition and precision, by conservation rather than innovation. Yet the theologians of the Second Reformation, as Alexander Mitchell, the great historian of the Westminster Assembly, calls it, believed that they were carrying on to completion the work that had been begun by Zwingli, Calvin, and Bullinger. In a very real sense the Westminster Confession was the product of one hundred and twenty-five years of theological work.

The place of the Confession in the history of Christian doctrine is such that a grasp of its significance is crucial for an understanding of the contemporary theological situation. The Confession was not only the conclusion of one hundred and twenty-five years of Protestant theology; it was also in a real sense, along with other seventeenth-century statements of the faith, the conclusion of sixteen centuries of theological work. The radical break in man's intellectual history occurred with the Enlightenment and the intellectual and social developments of the nineteenth century. The scientific revolution, the industrial revolution, the revolution in historical consciousness, the achievements of Darwin, Marx, Freud, Einstein, and many others fundamentally changed the way men thought of the world and related themselves to it. The writers of the Confession had far more in common with the men of the New Testament age than contemporary men have with the writers of the Confession. The Confession is, therefore, the last statement of the faith before the shattering intellectual and social experience of modern man.

Theological time, however, is not the same as chronological time. All men live in the same chronological time, but it has been possible for men in the twentieth century to live theologically in the seventeenth. In the twentieth century the words of the Confession have been repeated with nostalgic or desperate yearning for the theological assurances of the time before the break in man's intellectual history. On the other hand, the Confession has aroused the anger of those for whom it is the embodiment of an archaic and impossible theology. The nostalgia and the anger can both be understood, but neither provides a valid and constructive approach to the Confession. The purpose and the intentionality of the words of the Confession, written in the seventeenth century, are no longer the same today whether they are repeated in nostalgia or anger. A more constructive approach than either nostalgia or anger is first to seek to understand what the Confession was saying in its time, and secondly, to make use of it in the constructive repair and statement of theology today. The problems of contemporary theology are abundant evidence that theologians have not been able to articulate the faith in our time with the adequacy that writers of the Confession showed in their age that was then coming to an end. One precondition for theological depth and wisdom is always the recapitulation of the church's articulation of its faith in the past. Only those who have been able to live empathetically through the theology of the past and to identify with it are likely to be equipped to do constructive work in theology today.

The Westminster Confession is also an illustration of outstanding theological achievement and technical competence. The language is carefully defined and precise. It holds together with remarkable logical clarity and is true to all the theological angles and nuances. The Confession is amazingly complete and comprehensive. It combines doctrine and practice. No theology today achieves this high level of technical competence. Yet the irony of the Westminster Assembly's work was that its very greatness was its downfall. History soon demonstrated that the Confession was too precise and too comprehensive. It was more logical than either divine revelation or man's experience, and it claimed more assurance and knowledge than it was given man to know. In terms of the interpretive categories of Reinhold Niebuhr, the historical destiny of the Westminster Assembly's theological work was to be neither pathetic nor tragic, but ironic.[4] Certainly the Westminster Confession is in no sense pathetic or weak. It represents theology of such technical competence that it has seldom been equaled, much less surpassed. Neither is the Confession tragic. It is no final defiance of the brute facts of existence, nor is there any conscious sense of failure or an inability to articulate faith. Yet its fate has been ironic. Just as the strong man's strength becomes his undoing because he trusts it too much, so the very achievements of the Westminster Confession contained hidden flaws that were its undoing.

The theologian never triumphs, and his works are always incomplete and flawed. The theological enterprise is an endless pilgrimage or dialogue. Every theological achievement opens up new possibilities. And likewise every theological statement is finite, limited by a particular time and place. The theologian lives and is justified by faith, not by sight. And his pilgrimage or dialogue is endless. The theologians of the Westminster Assembly, for all their competence, and their Confession and Catechisms, for all their excellence, are no exceptions. For this reason the Confession illustrates both the achievements and the perils of the theological enterprise.

PART I
BACKGROUND AND CONTEXT

The Historical Character of Creeds

One of the most significant intellectual movements of the past two centuries has been the development of historical thinking. Men think historically when they perceive that human achievements do not simply have a history, but that they grow out of history, are dependent upon history, and are unintelligible apart from their own historical context. With this new sense of history new methods of historical study have developed. These new methods of analysis and criticism enable men to discover "what has actually happened" in contrast to what is thought to have happened. This is the goal of all good history, even though no historical work ever fully achieves it. The improvements in the historians' craft, which became increasingly better during the nineteenth century, are a great gain, though the results of historical scrutiny have sometimes upset cherished ideas about the past. But perhaps the most significant change that historical thinking or consciousness has brought about is a new awareness that human achievements grow out of a particular history and are limited by that history.

No one would or could write the Westminster Confession today just as it was written in 1644–1647. It is possible of course to take the Confession as it was written, and, by an act of will, repeat it today. But if it had not been written, no group of men could write it today just as it was written then. However, this does not mean that the Confession of the seventeenth century is useless to us now. A contemporary man can affirm the Confession by acknowledging that if he had been a member of the Assembly, confronted by the same issues and with the same resources available to him, he would have said very much what the Assembly affirmed in the Confession. Moreover, he can also affirm that what the Westminster Assembly said in its particular historical situation, he must substantially affirm in a way appropriate to his own situation. There is continuity as well as discontinuity within history. If there are no perennial theologies that can simply be repeated from one age to another, there are perennial human

problems; and the Christian also believes that, though his apprehension of the truth of God is always historically conditioned,
God himself is not limited by man's partial and fragmentary
vision.

The same historical consciousness that makes us aware that
the Westminster Confession grew out of the particular historical
context of the seventeenth century should also make us aware
that our present theological achievements and insights are conditioned by our own particular time. The fact that the Westminster
Confession is a historical and human achievement does not
downgrade it, for the same historical consciousness ought to
make us critical of the assumptions of our own age. The achievements of the past are correctives and guides that theologians
today must take seriously as they go about their tasks. As a historical achievement, the Westminster Confession should be neither absolutized nor rejected. It should be accepted for what it
is, a remarkable theological achievement of the Reformed community in the seventeenth century, and received with gratitude
for the guidance that it may give for the theological task today.

The historical character of the theological enterprise is very
tantalizing. There is a human desire for certainty and perma-
nence. Men want a creed that will supersede all creeds, that will
be irreformable and infallible. Yet the Reformed community has
always rejected the notion that any one creed can be elevated to
an exclusive position in the life of the church. The very fact of
multiple creeds bears witness to the limited and finite character
of all creeds, though certainly some creeds are better than others.
When a movement for a universal, Reformed creed arose in the
Presbyterian Alliance in 1925, Karl Barth pointed out the radically historical character of all theology and especially of Reformed creeds. "A Reformed Creed is *the statement, spontaneously
and publically formulated by a Christian community within a geograph-
ically limited area, which, until further action, defines its character to
outsiders; and which, until further action, gives guidance for its own doctrine and life; it is a formulation of the insight currently given to the whole
Christian Church by the revelation of God in Jesus Christ, witnessed to by
Holy Scriptures alone.*"[1]

Barth's conviction that theology is written for today, not for the future, for time, not for eternity, is surely applicable to the creedal enterprise. This fact was understood clearly enough by the Reformers. When Bullinger and Jud signed the First Helvetic Confession, they made this comment: "We wish in no way to prescribe for all churches through these articles a single rule of faith. For we acknowledge no other rule of faith than Holy Scripture. We agree with whoever agrees with this, although he uses different expressions from our Confession. For we should have regard for the fact itself and for the truth, not for the words. We grant to everyone the freedom to use his own expressions which are suitable for his church and will make use of this freedom ourselves, at the same time defending the true sense of the Confession against distortions."[2] Bullinger and Jud would accept the creed for what it was, a useful but broken and limited attempt to state the Christian faith in a particular time and place.

In actual practice, the Reformed churches wrote confessions whenever the occasion arose. More than fifty creedal statements of some importance were officially formulated by Reformed communities during the 125 years preceding Westminster.[3] There was no necessity for this proliferation of creeds. Reformed churchmen deliberately chose to write new creeds, sometimes in very tense situations as in Scotland, even when existing creeds were available. They confessed the faith as they knew it in a particular time and place. They refused to exalt any one creed as the perennial theology of the church or as a theology for eternity. They knew that every statement of faith is very historical and limited by the finiteness and sin of man.

The Lutheran situation was different.[4] They had creedal documents written, except for the Formula of Concord, by two men, Martin Luther and Philip Melanchthon, living in one geographical area in the space of eight years. It is possible to speak of the theology of the Lutheran confessional statements, but the Reformed confessions are too diverse to allow one to speak of *the* Reformed theology.[5] There were Reformed Christians then as now who coveted the Lutheran creedal situation. Yet even in 1581, when the creedal unity of the Lutherans was impressive with the recent adoption of the Book of Concord, the Reformed community refused to adopt one creed and settled for a harmony of existing confessions.[6]

This early position in regard to creeds had begun to fade in the seventeenth century with the increased standardization of theological method and terminology, and with the increasing concerns of orthodoxy to purify the faith and to protect and preserve it. After the work of the Westminster Assembly, the process was intensified by the very nature of the Confession and the Catechisms. The Confession quickly became magisterial, normative theology in English-speaking Calvinism.

The style and character of the Confession and Catechisms obscure their historical character. They contain a few references to the concrete facts of history, such as the vigorous indictment of the "papists" and the division of mankind into superiors, inferiors, and equals. For the most part, the language of the Confession is logical, technical, and abstract. The historical character and language of the Bible and of many Reformed creeds were deliberately rejected. Theology for the sake of preciseness was abstracted as far as possible from history and experience. Hence the style of the Confession and Catechisms tempted the reader to exempt this theology from the ambiguities and the relativities of all historical enterprises. Many did conclude that there was a perennial theology that was equally good in all times and places.

Closer examination, however, reveals that the abstract style and the logical precision betray the place of the Confession in history. Even though the members of the Assembly carried on their work in isolation from many of the very significant scientific, philosophical, and political events, their style dates them. Anyone knowing the Confession and the Catechisms and the era, especially the era that was at its climax, could date the documents with relative precision. For this reason it is important to point out some of the historical factors that were of great importance in the writing of the Confession and Catechisms.

The historical study of the Westminster Confession contributes to its contemporary usefulness in two ways. First of all, historical study enables the modern reader to understand what the Confession actually says, and it clears away calumnies and misinterpretations. All students of the Confession are indebted to such scholars as Alex. F. Mitchell, whose study of the Confession opened it to readers in a way that is only possible for one who has studied the deliberations of the Assembly. Mitchell was especially concerned to point out that the Confession did not represent an extreme version of the Reformed faith. He argued that the writers of the Confession did not necessarily take the six days of creation as literal, twenty-four-hour days, that the Confession did not necessarily teach a limited atonement or that some children dying in infancy were damned, that the Confession was not as negative toward those who had never heard of the gospel, as it might seem.[7] Mitchell's studies did resolve some of the problems that a modern man in the nineteenth century had with the Confession.

Today the problem is deeper, for men living in the last third of the twentieth century have far less in common with the culture of the 1640's than did those who lived in the last third of the nineteenth century. The problem that a contemporary reader has with the Westminster Confession is not with particular items in the Confession but with the idiom and the cultural perspective of the entire Confession. The only way in which the Westminster Confession can be a truly significant statement of the faith today is through an understanding of its historical nature. When the Confession is understood as a magnificent statement of the faith in its particular context, then it becomes a clue and guide to the articulation of the faith in the contemporary culture with its peculiar issues, questions, and challenges. Historical study must provide help not only for understanding what the Confession says, but also for determining how what it actually says was elicited, shaped, and conditioned by its particular place in history.

THE POLITICAL CONTEXT

The Westminster Assembly was the product not simply of the internal theological life of the church, but also of the economic, social, and political forces of the time. While it is impossible to ignore the religious factors that were involved in the upheavals of English history in the 1640's and 1650's, recent studies have made it apparent that the term *Puritan Revolution* has to be qualified. Economic factors such as prices and land, political factors such as the increased power of Parliament or the converging of the interests of the gentry with the Puritan preachers, international factors such as the threat of continental powers played their parts, not only for English Protestants but also for English traders.[1]

The political preparation that preceded the Westminster Assembly was deliberate, partly from choice and partly from the force of events. The origins of the Westminster Assembly reach far back into the Puritan movement and especially into the conflict between the Puritans and the Stuart kings, James I and Charles I.[2] The immediate background includes Charles' attempt to force the prayer book on the Church of Scotland in 1637 as part of his effort to bring the Church of Scotland into conformity with the Episcopal Church of England. This led to the National Covenant in Greyfriar's churchyard in Edinburgh (1638), to the General Assembly of the Church of Scotland (1638) that protested the policies of Charles, and subsequently to the First Bishops' War when Charles attempted to put down the Scottish rebellion. Charles now had to call Parliament to raise funds, but Charles adjourned Parliament when it began listing its grievances. The controversy with the Scots continued and the Second Bishops' War broke out in 1640. Scottish troops marched into England. Charles was forced once again to call Parliament in November 1640. This Parliament continued in session until it was purged by Cromwell in 1648 and dispersed by him in 1653. Parliament was also in conflict with the King on religious as well as political and social grounds, and it regarded the invading

Scottish army as an ally. This controversy erupted in a struggle that would continue until the King had been executed in 1649 and the Protectorate established in 1653. The controversy between King and Parliament was rooted in the deep-seated religious, social, and political ferment in the whole of society. In the Root and Branch petition of 1640 a long list of theological and ecclesiastical grievances was presented Parliament by his majesty's subjects in London and in several counties of the kingdom.[3] Subsequently numerous petitions calling for reformation and for a synod to deal with the religious situation were presented. On December 1, 1641, the House of Commons presented the King with the Grand Remonstrance, which outlined many of the theological and ecclesiastical grievances and called for a synod. "And the better to effect the intended reformation, we desire there may be a general synod of the most grave, pious, learned and judicious divines of this island; assisted with some from foreign parts, professing the same religion with us, who may consider all things necessary for the peace and good government of the Church, and represent the results of their consultations unto the Parliament, to be there allowed of and confirmed, and receive the stamp of authority, thereby to find passage and obedience throughout the kingdom."[4] In April 1642, Parliament began the selection of members for the prospective Assembly. In May 1642, a bill was introduced in Parliament calling for an Assembly, but the King withheld his approval. In June 1643, both houses of Parliament, disregarding the refusal of the King, agreed upon an ordinance calling the Assembly into existence. The ordinance is specific as to the task of the Assembly and as to its limitations.

> Whereas, amongst the infinite blessings of Almighty God upon this nation, none is or can be more dear unto us than the purity of our religion; and for that, as yet, many things remain in the Liturgy, Discipline, and Government of the Church, which do necessarily require a further and more perfect reformation than as yet hath been attained; and whereas it hath been declared and resolved by the Lords and Commons assembled in Parliament, that the present Church-government by archbishops, bishops, their chancellors, commissaries, deans, deans and chapters, archdeacons, and other

ecclesiastical officers depending upon the hierarchy, is evil, and justly offensive and burdensome to the kingdom, a great impediment to reformation and growth of religion, and very prejudicial to the state and government of this kingdom; and that therefore they are resolved that the same shall be taken away, and that such a government shall be settled in the Church as may be most agreeable to God's holy word, and most apt to procure and preserve the peace of the Church at home, and nearer agreement with the Church of Scotland, and other Reformed Churches abroad; and, for the better effecting hereof, and for the vindicating and clearing of the doctrine of the Church of England from all false calumnies and aspersions, it is thought fit and necessary to call an Assembly of learned, godly, and judicious Divines, who, together with some members of both the Houses of Parliament, are to consult and advise of such matters and things, touching the premises, as shall be proposed unto them by both or either of the Houses of Parliament, and to give their advice and counsel therein to both or either of the said Houses, when, and as often as they shall be thereunto required: . . .

. . . the said persons, or so many of them as shall be so assembled or sit, shall have power and authority, and are hereby likewise enjoined, from time to time during this present Parliament, or until further order be taken by both the said Houses, to confer and treat among themselves of such matters and things, touching and concerning the Liturgy, Discipline, and Government of the Church of England, or the vindicating and clearing of the doctrine of the same from all false aspersions and misconstructions, as shall be proposed unto them by both or either of the said Houses of Parliament, and no other; and to deliver their opinions and advices of, or touching the matters aforesaid, as shall be most agreeable to the word of God, to both or either of the said Houses, from time to time, in such manner and sort as by both or either of the said Houses of Parliament shall be required; and the same not to divulge, by printing, writing, or otherwise, without the consent of both or either House of Parliament.

. . . That this Ordinance, or any thing therein contained, shall not give unto the persons aforesaid, or any of them, nor shall they in this Assembly assume to exercise any jurisdiction, power, or authority ecclesiastical whatsoever, or any other power than is herein particularly expressed.[5]

The Assembly convened on July 1, 1643, in the face of a prohibition and warning by Charles I, with a sermon by the

Prolocutor (presiding officer), William Twisse. The first work of
the Assembly was a revision of the Thirty-Nine Articles in order
to remove any possibility of Arminian, Pelagian, or Roman interpretation.[6]

Arminianism and Romanism were slogans that connoted
quite as much as they denoted. Arminianism gets its name from
Arminius, the Dutch theologian who sought to modify the doctrine of predestination that was held by Reformed orthodoxy; but
English Arminianism cannot be identified with the views of Arminius. It did emphasize human freedom and tended, as Tuckney
charged, to make the love of God so free as to made it shallow.[7]
But Arminianism was also identified with a more relaxed attitude
toward theology and also toward the discipline of the Christian
life. It was likewise associated with episcopacy and the divine
right of kings. Pelagianism was closely related to Arminianism in
popular theology, though Arminius had been careful to define his
doctrine in distinction from Pelagianism, insisting that man could
not turn to God without divine grace. Pelagius, in his controversy
with Augustine in the fifth century, had exalted man's freedom
and his capacity to respond to the love of God. He denied original sin, and he limited grace to revelation and man's created
capacities. Romanism specifically referred to those elements in
the liturgy and government of the church that the Puritans did
not feel had been sufficiently reformed. It too had political implications. There were Roman Catholics with great influence in
the government, and many hoped England would be a Catholic
nation again. The role of Catholics in government was also a
sensitive issue in foreign policy, especially when Holland, with
which many English sympathized, was still in conflict with Catholic Spain. Furthermore, the Thirty Years War, which Protestants
understood as an effort to exterminate the Protestant community, was still in process when the Assembly met. Arminianism
and Romanism had specific theological references, but they also
had a range of social and political implications that a secular
culture such as ours finds difficulty understanding. The effort to
eliminate any remnants of either from the confession of the
church was directed to a broad range of concerns and would

orient the whole work of the Assembly. By October 12 the revision of the first fifteen Articles had been completed and work had begun on the sixteenth.[8] The work was never completed, but the debates and discussions served as a useful foundation for the later work on the Confession and Catechisms.

A new situation that had long been anticipated, and hoped for by some, was the occasion of another assignment. Parliament, faring badly in the war with the King during the summer of 1643, needed the support of Scotland. On August 17 a Solemn League and Covenant was approved by the Scottish Parliament, and in September it was approved by the English Parliament. The object of the Solemn League and Covenant was the defense and "preservation of the reformed religion in the Church of Scotland in doctrine, worship, discipline, and government, . . . [and] the reformation of religion in the kingdoms of England and Ireland . . . according to the Word of God, and the examples of the best reformed Churches, and [the bringing of] the Churches of God in the three kingdoms to the nearest conjunction of uniformity in religion, confession of faith, form of Church government, directory for worship and catechising . . ."[9] On September 25, 1643, members of the Assembly and the Scottish commissioners subscribed the Solemn League and Covenant.[10] From this point the Assembly took a new direction.

The Solemn League and Covenant meant that the Assembly would devote a major proportion of its time to church government and worship. In these areas members of the Assembly had their deepest differences. In the end the Assembly drew up a Form of Presbyterial Government in which the Presbyterianism of Melville, Cartwright, and Travers was tempered both by the Congregationalists and by the Erastians who insisted that the church's power was limited to moral persuasion.[11] It also replaced the *Book of Common Prayer* with a Directory for Worship, that, in place of fixed forms, contained directions for worship, some of which were compromises or were ambiguous. The real consensus of the Assembly was in the area of theology, and in the Confession and Catechisms it reached its highest technical achievement.

It is important to note that the Assembly was an appointment of Parliament, not an ecclesiastical synod. Its purpose was to advise Parliament, not to act in the name of the church. Its charter allowed it no freedom of initiative and permitted advice only on such things as were proposed to the Assembly by Parliament. Members were not to divulge by printing or writing or otherwise their proceedings except with permission of Parliament. The Assembly was explicitly prohibited from assuming "to exercise any jurisdiction, power, or authority ecclesiastical whatsoever."[12] The members were appointed by Parliament. The lay members attended as members of Parliament, not as church officers, except for the Scottish lay commissioners. Robert Baillie, a Scottish commissioner, observed, " . . . this is no proper Assembly, but a meeting called by the Parliament to advise them in what things they are asked . . ."[13]

The Assembly carried on its theological work, however, in splendid isolation from the political and social events of the time. There is no indication that the members were put under any political pressure on theological issues. This was due to the theological consensus that was shared by the theologians and their culture. It does not mean that the theology was indifferent to political and social crises. The preaching of the members of the Assembly to Parliament and to the public always included political and social applications. Indeed, seldom has preaching been so directly applied to the events of the day. The members of the Assembly understood the happenings of their time in terms of their theology and the providence of God, and they believed that God would fulfill his purposes in England either through reform or through apocalyptic events.

CHRONOLOGY

(Many histories report events of these years concisely and clearly. The following dates help to keep events in order.)

1603	Accession of James I
1625	Accession of Charles I
1637	Imposition of Prayer Book on Church of Scotland
1639	First Bishops War requires King to call "Short" Parliament. (1640)
1640	Second Bishops War. Scottish army marches into England.
November 1640	King compelled to call Long Parliament.
December 1640	London Petition, calling for abolishment of episcopacy, root, and branches
November 1641	Parliament passes Grand Remonstrance.
May 13, 1643	Ordinance calling for Assembly introduced in the Commons. Passes June 12, 1643.
July 1, 1643	Assembly convened.
August 17, 1643	Solemn League and Covenant approved by Scottish Parliament.
September 1643	Solemn League and Covenant approved by English Parliament.
September 25, 1643	Members of Assembly and Parliament and Scottish Commissioners subscribe to Solemn League and Covenant.
July 8– October 12, 1643	Revision of first fifteen of Thirty-Nine Articles
1643–1644	Work began on Form of Government and Directory of Worship.
August 20, 1644	Committee appointed on Confession of Faith.

November 26, 1646	Confession of Faith finished and presented to Parliament on December 4–7, 1646.
April 5, 1647	Minutes note that Confession finished with proof texts.
April 26, 1647	Scripture proofs for Confession given to Parliament.
August 27, 1647	Confession approved by Church of Scotland.
October 15, 1647	Larger Catechism completed.
November 25, 1647	Shorter Catechism presented to House of Commons.
April 14, 1648	Catechisms presented in final forms.
1648	Purge of Parliament by Oliver Cromwell
February 22, 1649	Last numbered Plenary Session of the Assembly
February 22, 1649–March 25, 1652	Members of the Assembly met occasionally to examine and license candidates for the ministry.
December 1653	Oliver Cromwell proclaimed Lord Protector.

The Cultural Context

The Westminster Assembly met at the end of one age and at the beginning of another. The seventeenth century marks both the decisive divide in the history of Christian thought and the beginning of the modern era. Many of the forces and ideas that have shaped the modern world were already at work in 1643. Indeed, members of the Assembly were aware, at least intellectually, of these factors. But insofar as the minutes of the Assembly reveal the concerns of the members, they were not moved by these forces, except to deny or to refute them.

The world, for the members of the Westminster Assembly, was God-centered. The great question was still, "How shall a man be saved?" When the armies of Parliament fared badly, members of the Assembly did not ask about military strategy or supplies, but about the providence of God. The kind of truth that interested the members of the Assembly was metaphysical and theological. They asked "Why?" rather than "How?" Though they knew about Copernicus, they lived and theologized in terms of the old geocentric world in which theology could easily be imagined in spacial terms.

Order was a dominant characteristic of the world in which the Assembly lived. It was the order guaranteed by the creative power and wisdom of God and maintained by his all-wise providence, in spite of man's sin. In this ordered world of the great chain of being, everything had its place.[1] There was a certain glory of the divine wisdom in every place, however humble. The authors of the Catechisms could speak of superiors, inferiors, and equals with none of the bad conscience that such a division of mankind arouses even in the calloused today. The surds, the chaotic events, even the mystery of human freedom in which existentialists exult today were foreign to the common experience of the men of the Assembly. It is not strange that in this well-ordered and rational world Thomas Aquinas' theology was read. For Thomas the world was also well-ordered and rational. Man by his mind could think the world and move by inference

from the contingent being of human experience to the necessary
being that is God.

There is a certain tension between a doctrine of the sovereignty of God and the ordered universe of the great chain of
being. The personal, acting God of the Old Testament too easily
upset the orders of men and even of creation. It may be argued
that God, as he is known in the Confession, is "ordered" by all
the attributes that are ascribed to him in Chapter II of the Confession. Nevertheless, any theology with so strong a doctrine of
predestination and providence is precariously related to the "ordered" universe. In part the "ordered" universe broke because
of the pressures of the new age, perhaps chiefly so; but there were
some who broke up the orders of the world because they believed
that God willed its judgment. The tension between the personal
Almighty God of the Biblical tradition and the "ordered universe" is implicit in the Confession but not explicit.

In such an intellectual climate it is clear that there is a closer
relationship between the rational theology of Lord Herbert of
Cherbury (1583–1648) and the theology of the Assembly than at
first seems to be the case. The Assembly's theologians began with
the Bible as the given source of theology, and Lord Herbert
began with what he considered the common experience or no-
tions of man. From this point on, however, there is a remarkable
similarity in their theological methodologies.[2]

The Cambridge Platonists were not represented at the Assembly, but some of the most influential members of the Assembly were their friends. Tuckney and Arrowsmith were notably in
communication with Benjamin Whichcote. The Cambridge
Platonists rejected the Puritan theology of the members of the
Assembly, and it is easy to note the difference in their writings.
The Platonists were more open and free. They sought to hold
reason and faith together and refused to set the rational in opposition to the spiritual. Natural and revealed religion differed only
in way of descent. They perceived a unity and harmony in life in
which man's truths and experiences participated, and they did
not wish to fragment what God had joined together. Their emphasis on reason led to a concern for toleration, as man must not

be coerced in the search for truth. They wanted to free religion from narrow, bitter spirits. There were clear differences between the Platonists and Puritans, as Whichcote and Tuckney perceived in their letters; but in the perspective of history they were both rationalists, with inordinate confidence in the power of the human reason to know reality and to know God. Tuckney's theology was shaped more by the classical Protestant tradition with its emphasis upon Scripture and the Christian revelation, but in the working out of his theology he shared many common assumptions with the Platonists.[3]

Basil Willey has commented concerning the Cambridge Platonists that in the field of theology ". . . we must expect to find the rationalisers largely concerned with putting an *idea*, and *abstraction*, where formerly there had been a *picture*. For only the abstract, only what could be conceptually stated, could claim to be *real*: all else was shadow, image, or at least 'type' or symbol."[4] These same observations apply equally to the theology of the Westminster Assembly.

The most important aspect of the cultural context of the Assembly is the breakup of the ideas and forces that had formed the intellectual world of the Assembly. A "transfer of interest" had taken place from metaphysics and theology to experiment and observation, from the "why" questions to the "how" questions. Men did not refute old, established ideas but became absorbed in new questions and concerns. As Herbert Butterfield has pointed out, Galileo (1564–1642) did not refute Aristotle's concept of motion. He simply ignored what Thomas Aquinas had said and sought to observe how things in motion behaved. The new man, who was just beginning to emerge when the Assembly met, was less and less asking why things happened, and asking how they happened, and how they could be controlled.[5]

New movements were at work in philosophy. Bacon (1561–1626) had emphasized the role of experiment and observation in knowledge. Ramus (1515–1572), who died in the massacre of St. Bartholomew's Day, had challenged the binding role of authority and had likewise placed new emphasis on experience. Descartes' controversy with Voetius had broken out in Holland in 1649. His

Discourse on Method was published in 1637 and was available in England before the Assembly met. Descartes raised doubt to the level of methodology; the way to truth is through doubt. Abelard had proposed something of the same method in theology in the twelfth century. Descartes' method was no less at variance with the theological method of the Assembly than Abelard's had been with Bernard's, the saintly but orthodox and conservative, twelfth-century churchman. However, the general climate of opinion was more favorable to Descartes than to Abelard.[6]

Men were also aware, as they had not been, of the existence of non-Christian religions. The very fact that the Assembly had to deal with this question in a brief and negative fashion indicates that this question was alive.[7] Tuckney discussed it at length in a sermon in which the traditionally orthodox answers were given.[8] This was also one of the primary concerns of Lord Herbert of Cherbury.[9] On this issue, as on others, the Assembly was not really alive in any positive way to the new forces that were developing.

The sociological context of the Assembly was Christendom or "Protestantdom." However, the movements that would increasingly shape a secular society were already at work. Members of the Assembly were themselves, in contradiction of their intentions, contributing to the emergence of the new concept of denominations.[10] Yet the members of the Assembly could not imagine the culture that would soon emerge, a culture in which men would be free to reject Christian presuppositions. In such a culture, theology would finally be forced to deal with questions men asked from outside the circle of faith and to face the judgment of those who rejected both Christian theology and ethics. At the time of the Reformation, Calvin had been alive to the great creative forces of humanism, and he did not seek to isolate himself as a theologian from these forces. By the time of Westminster, orthodox theology was already being carried on in isolation from the intellectual currents of the day. After Westminster, as society became increasingly secular, orthodoxy would finally become very defensive in its intellectual isolation. Theology had already begun to develop according to its own internal principles

which were not in dialogue with the world, and among the orthodox it would continue to do so for a long time.

Modern science was born in the seventeenth century in the
fusion of mathematics and experiment.[11] In fact, Whitehead has
called the seventeenth century the century of genius.[12] Newton
was born in and Galileo died in 1642 just as the arrangements for
the Westminster Assembly were being completed. During the
lifetimes of these two men the three laws of motion and the law
of gravitation were worked out. Whitehead comments: ". . . the
lives of Descartes and Huyghens fall within the period occupied
by these great terminal figures. The issue of the combined labours of these four men has some right to be considered as the
greatest single intellectual success which mankind has
achieved."[13] In addition, seventeenth-century England produced
Harvey, Boyle, and Ray, pioneers in physiology, chemistry, and
botany respectively. The Royal Society had its origin about 1645,
precisely while the Assembly was meeting. At least two of the
original nucleus of the Society were associated with the Assembly: Wallis who was a secretary of the Assembly and the first
commentator on the Shorter Catechism, and Theodore Haak
who was employed by the Assembly to translate a Dutch commentary on the Bible.[14] The strong Puritan character of the Royal
Society has been noted by Douglas Bush: "Even the Royal Society of 1662 had a strong Puritan tinge. There were general
affinities between Baconian science and rational Puritanism: im-
patience of traditional authority and useless learning; the critical
and empirical instinct; the ideal of action rather than contemplation; belief in utility, progress, and reform, in the study of God's
creation and in 'works' as a religious and humanitarian duty and
pleasure; and—what is not really inconsistent with that—the dis-
position to segregate the religious and the secular, the divine and
the 'natural'. . . . It goes without saying that this active Puritan
and middle-class sympathy with science contained no suspicion
of the irreligious philosophy associated with Hobbes."[15]

The critical point that must be noted is the theological isolation of the work of the Assembly from the issues that were surely
latent in the scientific development that had begun with Coper-

nicus' publication, *De Revolutionibus Orbium Caelestium,* in 1543. In the second half of the seventeenth century, theologians such as Richard Bentley and scientists, no less than Boyle and Newton, did try to relate theology and science.[16] They used science in the defense of the faith as members of the Assembly felt no obvious need of doing. Perhaps it was impossible for an Assembly meeting just at the moment when the theocentric world of Christendom and the vision of the Holy Community were at their climax to be aware of the significance of the new science. Within twenty years it was painfully obvious to Milton and to others that the Holy Community had failed, and within a century and a half it was painfully obvious to Schleiermacher that a host of theological problems confronted the Christian community. The primary reason for relating the Westminster Assembly to the events that were taking place is not to blame the Assembly, especially for failure to achieve insights that were historically impossible, but to assess the Assembly's place in the history of Christian thought and to understand better its unique contributions as well as its flaws.

THE THEOLOGICAL CONTEXT

The Assembly was the beneficiary of almost 125 years of Protestant theology. It was aware of this heritage. On the one hand, it was determined to avoid innovation in theology. It did not cherish novelty. On the other hand, it was aware of a need for a "further and more perfect reformation than as yet hath been attained."[1] This reformation was a *purification*, not a change of the Reformed faith. The conservation of the theological work of the past century, not originality, was to be the hallmark of the Assembly.

Reformed theology had achieved an amazing consensus during the first half of the seventeenth century. This was due to the network of communication that had always existed between the Reformed communities of Britain and the continent, and to the catechisms and compendiums that summarized the Reformed faith in compact, brief propositions that were designed to aid the memory. *The Compendium of Christian Theology* by Johannes Wollebius (1586–1629) was published in 1626, and while not translated into English until 1650, it still serves as an illustration of the brief, clear, and positive way in which Reformed theology was popularized and universalized in the Reformed communities of Britain and the continent.

Theological controversies were being resolved, as the issues of divine sovereignty and human freedom had been at the Synod of Dort (1619), in favor of a moderate position that could claim the allegiance of most theologians. In England the Puritans were indefatigable preachers, lecturers, and teachers who increasingly popularized a common theological vocabulary.[2] The phrases of the Westminster Shorter Catechism can be duplicated phrase by phrase from earlier catechisms.[3] Yet this was not the result of a compilation so much as it was of the theological consensus that had made these phrases the common vocabulary of theologians and laymen alike. In the increasingly pluralistic culture of our time, it is difficult to imagine the power of such a common theological vocabulary and commitment.

The theological debates were about fine points. Members of the Assembly did argue whether the atonement was accomplished by Christ's passive obedience on the cross which cancelled man's guilt or whether the atonement also included Christ's active obedience which was imputed to man as positive righteousness.[4] They likewise disputed about the order of the divine decrees, about the way God thought of man when he elected him to his eternal destiny.[5] The Supralapsarians said that God first elected some men to eternal life and that creation, the fall, and redemption followed to that end. The Infralapsarians objected that God thought of man as created and fallen, and then he elected some out of the mass of perdition to eternal life and to this end provided redemption in Christ. A third point of view was not vocably represented in the Assembly. According to this position, God, seeing men as created, fallen, and redeemed, elected those who believed in Christ to eternal life.

The major issues had been decided. The language of theology had been sharpened in lengthy debates and in treatises over many years and in many places. The consequence of this heritage is the precision, clarity, comprehension, and confidence of the Confession and Catechisms. Here we have the theological climax of a very great theological era.

The members of the Assembly deliberately sought to avoid the peculiar theologies of particular schools. They intended to give expression to a generic Reformed faith that could be agreed upon by the Reformed everywhere. They consciously sought the approval of the Reformed communities of the continent as well as Britain. During the debate on the decrees of God, Edward Reynolds, one of the most influential writers of the Confession, exclaimed, "Let not us put in disputes and scholastical things into a Confession of Faith."[6]

The Assembly drew upon a broad theological base. Multiple theological traditions were melded in the Puritan theological consensus. First there was the notable and ancient British theological tradition. This tradition had always been characterized by a strong Biblical understanding of reality. Meyrick H. Carré in his survey of British thought points out that the dynamic, personal

understanding of reality to be found in the Bible had shaped
British thought from the cloister schools of Jarrow (seventh century) and York (eighth century) to the universities of the sixteenth century. "The numerous philosophies of these centuries
had been engaged above all in the task of understanding and of
justifying the universal religion. They were adapted in various
forms to a system of divine truths and the system provided a
chain of presuppositions that directed the forms by which experience was interpreted. The chief postulate was that the universe
had been fashioned by a personal God who had revealed himself
to men in specific ways; and the metaphysical doctrines of being,
creation, becoming and end, were consequences of this postulate."[7] This Biblical understanding of reality was supplemented
by an Augustinian theology that had been mediated through
Anselm, Bradwardine, and John Wycliffe.[8] Augustinianism
stressed the divine initiative—that God loves us and chooses us
before we love him and choose him, the bondage of man's sin,
and the understanding of truth that directs a man to search the
depths of his interior life if he is to encounter the Divine Reality.
The works of Bradwardine had been edited by William Twisse
who was the Prolocutor of the Assembly.[9] In addition, the writing
of members of the Assembly abounds in quotations from Augustine.[10] The Confession's emphasis upon the Divine Sovereignty
and God's personal control of the world and human destiny did
not depend simply upon the writings of John Calvin but first of
all upon Augustine from whom Calvin himself learned much of
his theology. A third element in the British intellectual tradition
that Carré emphasizes was its empirical bent, which in the first
part of the sixteenth century was renewed by the writings of
Francis Bacon.[11] The awareness that thought must be tied to
concrete experience certainly influenced the theology of members of the Assembly, though, as we shall see later, the failure of
the writers of the Confession to keep their theology tied to experience was in part their undoing.

   In addition to the native British theological tradition, the
writers of the Confession drew upon the Reformed traditions of
the continent.[12] Here too their sources were diverse. The English

Puritans had learned their theology in part from the Reformed
theologians of Zurich, especially Bullinger. During the reign of
Mary some had taken refuge there. The correspondence of English churchmen with theologians of German-speaking Switzer-
land is voluminous, indicating active participation of Bullinger
and others in the shaping of British Protestantism. In addition
Bullinger's sermons *The Decades* were required reading for British
clergy in the sixteenth century.[13] The influence of the Reformed
theology of Geneva supplemented and gained ascendancy over
that of Zurich in the latter part of the sixteenth century.[14] It has
frequently been noted that the writers of the 1640's do not quote
Calvin as frequently as might be anticipated, but due allowance
must be given to the pervasive printing of Calvin's works in
English during the preceding century. Professor Cremeans summarizes the evidence. "The *Short-Title Catalogue* . . . [which lists
books published in English between 1475 and 1640] lists ninety-
six different editions of the writings of Calvin and fifty of Beza's
writings. No other foreign divines have as many, Luther and
Bullinger being nearest with thirty-eight each. Archbishop Parker
had more books published than any other official of the Anglican
Church, and he had only ten to his credit. One or more of Calvin's works were published almost every year between 1548 and
1634. Between 1578 and 1581, six to eight were published every
year. Between 1548 and 1600 no other writer had nearly so many
publications in English as John Calvin had. Only in the early
seventeenth century was his record surpassed, and then it was by
William Perkins and Henry Smith, both Calvinists."[15] In addition
Calvin's *Institutes* became the recognized textbook of theology at
Cambridge and Oxford.[16]

The developing covenant theology of the Puritans was a
third basic influence upon the writers of the Confession in addition to the Biblical, Augustinian, empirical approach of the British tradition and to the Reformed theology of the continent.
Covenant theology had also developed on the continent, but the
main influence on the Assembly was from within its native British
tradition.

The members of the Assembly were generally committed to

the theology that had developed in the classical Reformed traditions. They were not so hospitable to two of the three creative
and liberalizing movements in Reformed theology during the
seventeenth century: Arminianism and the theology of Saumur.
British theologians had participated in the Synod of Dort. The
members of the Assembly were well aware of its work. While the
"ever-memorable" John Hales of Eton bade John Calvin good
night at Dort, his fellow Englishmen had not.[17] Arminianism,
with its emphasis on human freedom at the expense, its opponents said, of divine grace, had no perceptible influence on the
work of the Assembly, except negatively. The school of theology
at Saumur in France had sought to modify the high Calvinism of
Reformed orthodoxy in many ways. It wrestled with such problems as the inspiration of the Bible, the transmission of the consequences of Adam's sin to his descendants, as well as the perennial
problem of human freedom and divine grace. Members of the
Assembly were aware of the theological developments at Saumur, and some may have been moderated by Amyraldus' writings
on predestination; but the positive influence of the theology of
Saumur was not great.[18] The members of the Assembly were fully
committed to the Reformed consensus, and they had not yet
experienced the doubts and the problems that the developing
revolution in human thinking and experience would bring with
it.

   Covenant theology also sought to liberalize and humanize
the Reformed orthodoxy of the seventeenth century. Orthodoxy
had developed a doctrine of the divine decrees that carried the
theologian to the dizzy height of the mind of God. Only the very
"strong" could abide in such realms for long. Covenant theology
focused attention, not upon the decrees as they existed in the
mind of God, but upon the working out of the decrees in history
and in human experience. By incorporating covenant theology
into the Confession, the doctrine of the decrees was modified,
and attention was shifted to the concrete facts of experience.
John Calvin had insisted that knowledge of God and knowledge
of man were indissolubly related and that you could not say
anything about one without saying it about the other.[19] This is

as profound an observation as is to be found in theology and is
an illustration of Calvin's insight as a theologian. In the history
of doctrine when the theological attention becomes focused too
exclusively upon God or man, a counteracting movement is inevitable. Covenant theology represents this swing of the pendulum,
and it should be noted that it was the only liberalizing movement
of the seventeenth century that was incorporated into the normative, international Calvinism.

Another factor in the theological context of the Assembly's
work was the presence of Roman Catholicism on the continent.
Baillie's letters express the same concern about the fate of Protestantism, the Wars of Religion, and the role of Roman Catholicism that men in the twentieth century have known in the face
of national socialism, communism, and the spread of alien
faiths.[20] Moreover, the Council of Trent had provided Roman
Catholicism with a clear, precise, and exact statement of faith.
Baillie's letters indicate that Roman Catholicism was very much
in the minds of at least some of the members of the Assembly.

The Assembly was also concerned with local doctrinal aber-
rations such as Antinomianism, which especially attracted its attention.[21] The Antinomians were visible. They were so caught up
in the free grace of God and in the ecstasy of the Spirit that they
neglected discipline and law. If a man is in the state of grace, they
said, God sees no sin in him, even if he commits murder or gets
drunk. Thus the law became unnecessary for the believer. The
Puritan conscience, as well as Puritan theology, reacted with
vigor to any such notion. Consequently the Assembly gave careful attention to the sections of the Confession on sanctification
and good works. There were other deviations from the theological norm that also concerned the Assembly. George Gillespie,
one of the Scottish commissioners, reported to the General Assembly in Edinburgh that the "Confession of Faith is framed so
as its great use against the floods of heresies and errors that
overflow that land; nay, their intention of framing of it was to
meet with all the considerable Errors of the present time, the
Socinian, Arminian, Popish, Antinomian, Anabaptistian, Independent errors, etc."[22] Arminianism and Romanism, as has been

noted, were pervasive concerns of the whole Puritan movement. Socinianism, which denied the deity of Jesus Christ, had been a persistent though small movement for a century.[23] Anabaptist and Independent positions affected the doctrine of the church and sacraments primarily. Most of the doctrinal deviations were not serious threats or problems for the Assembly.

It is significant that members of the Assembly were theologically unaware of the cultural, philosophical, and scientific developments that were already raising new questions for the Christian community. As has been mentioned, the Assembly either ignored these developments or summarily dismissed them. Yet in the end they would prove far more serious than the intramural doctrinal problems with which the Assembly did concern itself. The only conclusion that seems possible is that the Westminster Assembly stands at the climax of an epoch, and that those members, who must have been aware of the changes that were underway, did not significantly relate these changes to the theological task.

The Members of the Assembly and Their Work

The humanity and the historical character of the Assembly is nowhere better documented than in its members and their work. The members were chosen by Parliament to represent the counties, the universities, and Parliament itself. The original appointments to the Assembly included ten members of the House of Lords, twenty members of the House of Commons and 121 divines.[1] Subsequent appointments were made to fill vacancies.

A majority of the Assembly were Presbyterians, though some were willing to admit elders only "in a prudential way."[2] Only two of the Episcopalians appointed attended. The Independents included the five signers of the *Apologetical Narration*, Thomas Goodwin, Nye, Burroughes, Simpson, and Bridge, and five or six others. The Erastians were few but very able: Lightfoot, Selden, Coleman. Three commissioners were ministers of the Reformed Church of France with charges in Canterbury and London.

The Scottish commissioners, in distinction from the English members of the Assembly, were elected by a church court, the General Assembly of the Church of Scotland, as ministers and elders. The Assembly would have preferred that they sit as members of the body, but they insisted that they participate as commissioners of a party to the Solemn League and Covenant.[3] This gave them the right to advise the Assembly on all issues and far more influence than they would have had as individual members of the Assembly. They were very able men. Alexander Henderson was one of Scotland's greatest churchmen. George Gillespie was a very able debater, ready to cross words with the scholarly Selden. Samuel Rutherford was a capable teacher of theology. Robert Baillie, as his letters indicate, was a masterful observer of events both in their local and in their wider settings; and he was the equal of a modern news reporter in his knowledge of inside "gossip" and politics. The ruling elders were likewise able men.

The evaluation of the Assembly's membership has varied. Baxter in his well-known encomium exclaimed that: ". . . as far as I am able to judge by the information of all history of that kind, and by any other evidences left us, the Christian world, since the days of the apostles, had never a synod of more excellent divines than this and the synod of Dort."[4] Others regarded them with contempt or scorn.[5] It is true that the Assembly did not include a theologian whose brilliance would entitle him to a great place in the history of thought. It is also true, however, that the Assembly was composed of highly competent men who were fully able to utilize the accumulated theological work of more than a century. They were not creative minds so much as summarizers and interpreters of the tradition. They were for the most part preacher-teachers who wrote not theological masterpieces but sermons and occasional theological treatises. On this level of theological work they are unsurpassed.

One of the typical and most important members of the Assembly was Anthony Tuckney (1599–1670). He was born in 1599 and was educated at Cambridge.[6] He became assistant to John Cotton at Boston, Lincolnshire, and after Cotton left for America, he was responsible for the congregation. He left in 1643 to attend the Westminster Assembly. He was subsequently Master of Emmanuel College, Master of St. John's College, and Regius Professor of Divinity. He was rejected after the Restoration but placed on a pension. Richard Baxter spoke of him as "over humble," but as professor at Cambridge he exhibited integrity and strength, giving grounds for the tradition that in the selection of Fellows he might be deceived as to the applicant's godliness but not as to his scholarship.[7]

Tuckney was very active in the work of the Assembly. He was a member of the committee to perfect the Confession,[8] and he has been judged by Dr. Carruthers to have been the most influential writer of the Shorter Catechism.[9] The remarkable exposition of the Decalogue in the Larger Catechism has been attributed primarily to him.[10]

After Tuckney's death, forty of his sermons were published by his son.[11] The sermons belie the criticisms that are sometimes made of the Westminster Confession. They are warm-hearted, practical, and strongly Biblical in character. Christian faith must be embodied in life. Propositions are never adequate statements of the faith. "Logic Rules do not circumscribe God, nor should our reason."[12] *"Theologia* is not *scienta speculativa* but *practica.* "[13] "Divinity is an art of living."[14] In death all learning is lost. The notes of scholars may do others some good, but they do not help the dead.[15] Tuckney apparently felt no contradiction between this understanding of the Christian life and of the theological task and the theology of the Confession.

Tuckney wrote out of the mainstream of the Reformed tradition. In the *Forty Sermons* he quotes Augustine and Calvin most frequently, but he also quotes Zanchius, P. Martyr, Diodati, Beza, Bullinger, Ecolampadius, and others as well.

Another typical member was John Arrowsmith, born in 1602. He had been a preacher but became successively Master of St. John's and Trinity Colleges and Professor of Divinity. Like Tuckney he left sermons and a short theological treatise, *A Chain of Principles.*[16] In this treatise he develops six aphorisms out of the thirty he had planned. His style, like that of Tuckney, is the language of human discourse more than of the scholar's study. The language and imagery convey concern with human life and the concrete realities of human and Christian experience. The role of Christian revelation as the starting point of theology is quite definite, but the God of Christian revelation is quite reasonable. Any man using his reason will acknowledge the Divine Reality, and the ways of God, while ultimately mysterious, are not a scandal to human reason. Predestination and reprobation are not explained away, but Arrowsmith, following Davenant, seeks to round·off as many sharp corners as possible. Davenant, according to Arrowsmith, handled predestination "modestly," and this apparently was Arrowsmith's own intention. Any modern reader is struck by the absence of any awareness of the absurdities, incongruities, and irrationalities of human experience. The modern reader is also impressed with the relative simplicity of the theological task when it is not complicated by modern issues arising from the social, historical, and natural sciences. Yet of greater significance for the understanding of the Confession is the congruity that Arrowsmith apparently experienced between the formulation of theology in the Confession and Catechisms and the

explication of the faith in his own lectures which are Biblical,
human, and obviously meaningful even when read with the consciousness of another culture.

John Dury was less typical of the Assembly than Tuckney and
Arrowsmith, but he illustrates the breadth of membership. Dury
is best known today as one of the great advocates of the unity of
the church in the seventeenth century.[17] In 1642 he was in The
Hague as chaplain to Mary, daughter of Charles I. The call of the
Westminster Assembly inspired him with new hope, and on June
28, 1643, he was appointed to the place made vacant by the death
of Calibute Downing. Dury regarded the Westminster Assembly
and the Solemn League and Covenant as a pledge of Christian
unity in Britain and of closer relations with the churches on the
continent. He intended to be a mediator between Independents
and Presbyterians. "My aim shall be none other, but to stir—
thoughts of brotherly kindness, of meekness and of peace; to the
end that some may be taken up, which will help to reconcile the
affections of many divided about circumstantials; to preserve and
keep entire the unity which remains about fundamentals; and to
prevent or cure the manifold misprisions, which increase our
confusions, and obstruct the remedies of our diseases."[18] Dury
was acquainted with the theological work that had been done in
Holland by Ames and Cocceius, but there is no indication of his
influence on theological deliberations of the Assembly. Dury's
spirit was much more liberal than that of the Assembly as a whole.
In 1648 he was publicly censured by the Assembly for his com-
mendation of the English translation of Jacob Acontius' *Satans
Stratagems.*[19]

John Wallis, like Dury, is best known not for his connection
with the Westminster Assembly but for his role in the development of science and the Royal Society.[20] He was a mathematician
of distinction whose writings have a significant place in the history of that discipline. He was one of the group that began meeting in London in 1645 to promote scientific discussion and that
in 1662 became the Royal Society. He was a friend of Boyle,
Gregory, and Newton. He served as an assistant in the work of
the Assembly, and while not a member of the Assembly, he con-

tributed significantly to its proceedings. He wrote the first commentary on the Shorter Catechism.[21]

Tuckney and Arrowsmith, Dury and Wallis are only illustrations of the men who composed the Assembly. There were many others like Selden, the learned orientalist, who often embarrassed the clergymen who read from their English Bibles by reminding them that the Hebrew was different.[22] Gataker was an accomplished exegete and one of the first to recognize the distinctive character of New Testament Greek.[23] Edward Reynolds was respected for his wisdom and judgment. Stephen Marshall was one of the greatest preachers of his day. The active members of the Assembly were very competent men, as competent as composed any synod in church history.

The men who composed the Assembly were, however, very human men sharing the limitations and frailties of all men. The very historical character of the Assembly is nowhere better revealed than in the way in which they carried on the work and the debates of the Assembly. The legend that the answer to the Catechism question "What is God?" was unexpectedly spoken by George Gillespie in prayer after frustrating theological debate has obscured the very human work of the Assembly. In fact Gillespie was not a member of the Assembly when the Catechism was prepared.[24]

It is true that Marshall prayed for two hours and that Arrowsmith preached for one hour, presumably to an attentive congregation. Baillie describes an eight-hour service: "After Dr. Twisse had begun with a brief prayer, Mr. Marshall prayed large two hours most divinely, confessing the sins of the members of the Assembly in a wonderfully pathetic and prudent way. After, Mr. Arrowsmith preached one hour; then a psalm; thereafter, Mr. Vines prayed near two hours, and Mr. Palmer preached one hour, and Mr. Seaman prayed near two hours, then a psalm. After Mr. Henderson brought them to a short sweet conference of the heart confessed . . . and other seen faults to be remedied, . . . Dr. Twisse closed with a short prayer and blessing. This day [Baillie said] was the sweetest that I have seen in England."[25] It is also true that members of the Assembly had to be reprimanded for being absent from prayer. On one occasion the Assembly adopted the following resolutions: "Ordered—that the members of the Assembly do not bring any books or papers to read privately in the Assembly during the sitting of the Assembly. Ordered—that the members of the Assembly do forbear private communication during the sitting of the Assembly. Ordered— that the members of the Assembly forbear going from one place to another in the Assembly."[26] On other occasions members had to be reprimanded for coming late and leaving early. Both Lightfoot and Baillie in their accounts complain of the tediousness of the debates and of occasional irascibility.[27] These facts do not so much condemn the Assembly as remind us of its very historical and human character.

Robert Baillie left a vivid description of the Assembly that helps us today to imagine the setting and nature of the proceedings.

> Here no mortal man may enter to see or hear, let be to sitt, without ane order in wryte from both Houses of Parliament . . . The like of that Assemblie I did never see, and, as we hear say, the like was never in England, nor any where is shortlie lyke to be. They did sit in Henry the 7th's Chappell, in the place of the Convocation; but since the weather grew cold, they did go to Jerusalem chamber, a fair roome in the Abbey of Westminster, about the bounds of the College fore-hall, but wyder. At the one end nearest the doore, and both sydes are stages of seats as in the new Assemblie-House at Edinburgh, but not so high; for there will be roome but for five or six score. At the upmost end there is a chaire set on ane frame, a foot from the earth, for the Mr. Proloqutor Dr. Twisse. Before it on the ground stands two chairs for the two Mr. Assessors, Dr. Burgess and Mr. Whyte. Before these two chairs, through the length of the roome, stands a table, at which sitt the two scribes, Mr. Byfield and Mr. Roborough. The house is all well hung [with tapestry], and hes a good fyre, which is some dainties at London. Foranent the table, upon the Proloqutor's right hand, there are three or four rankes of formes. On the lowest we five doe sit. Upon the other, at our backs, the members of Parliament deputed to the Assemblie. On the formes foranent us, on the Proloqutor's left hand, going from the upper end of the house to the chimney, and at the other end of the house, and backsyde of the table till it come about to our seats, are four or five stages of forms, whereupon their divines sitts as they

please; albeit commonlie they keep the same place. From the chimney to the door there are no seats, but a voyd for passage. The Lords of Parliament use to sit on chairs, in that voyd, about the fire. We meet every day of the week, but Saturday. We sitt commonlie from nine to one or two afternoon. The Proloqutor at the beginning and end hes a short prayer. The man, as the world knows, is very learned in the questions he hes studied, and very good, beloved of all, and highlie esteemed; but merelie bookish, and not much, as it seems, acquaint with conceived prayer, [and] among the unfittest of all the company for any action; so after the prayer he sitts mute. It was the canny convoyance of these who guides most matters for their own interest to plant such a man of purpose in the chaire. The one assessour, our good friend Mr. Whyte, hes keeped in of the gout since our coming; the other, Dr. Burgess, a very active and sharpe man, supplies, so farr as is decent, the Proloqutor's place. Ordinarlie there will be present above threescore of their divines. These are divided in three Committees; in one whereof every man is a member. No man is excluded who pleases to come to any of the three. Every Committee, as the Parliament gives order in wryte to take any purpose to consideration, takes a portion, and in their afternoon meeting prepares matters for the Assemblie, setts doune their minde in distinct propositions, backs their propositions with texts of Scripture. After the prayer, Mr. Byfield the scribe, reads the proposition and Scriptures, whereupon the Assemblie debates in a most grave and orderlie way. No man is called up to speak [as was then the custom in the Scotch Assembly]; bot who stands up of his own accord, he speaks so long as he will without interruption. If two or three stand up at once, then the divines confusedlie calls on his name whom they desyre to hear first: On whom the loudest and maniest voices calls, he speaks. No man speaks to any bot to the Proloqutor. They harangue long and very learnedlie. They studie the questions well before hand, and prepares their speeches; but withall the men are esceeding prompt, and well spoken. I doe marvell at the very accurate and extemporall replyes that many of them usuallie doe make. When, upon every proposition by itself, and on everie text of Scripture that is brought to confirme it, every man who will hes said his whole minde, and the replyes, and duplies, and triplies, are heard; then the most part calls, To the question. Byfield the scribe rises from the table, and comes to the Proloqutor's chair, who, from the scribe's book, reads the proposition, and says, as many as are in opinion that the question is well stated in the proposition, let them say I; when I is heard, he says, as many as think otherwise, say No. If the difference of I's and No's be cleare, as

usuallie it is, then the question is ordered by the scribes, and they
go on to debate the first Scripture alleadged for proof of the proposition. If the sound of I and No be near equall, then sayes the
Proloqutor, as many as say I, stand up; while they stand, the scribe
and others number them in their minde; when they sitt down, the
No's are bidden stand, and they likewise are numbered. This way
is clear enough, and saves a great deal of time, which we spend in
reading our catalogue. When a question is once ordered, there is no
more debate of that matter; but if a man will vaige, he is quicklie
taken up by Mr. Assessor, or many others, confusedlie crying, Speak
to order, to order. No man contradicts another expresslie by name,
bot most discreetlie speaks to the Proloqutor, and at most holds on
the generall, The Reverend brother, who latelie or last spoke, on
this hand, on that syde, above, or below. I thought meet once for
all to give yow a taste of the outward form of their Assemblie. They
follow the way of their Parliament. Much of their way is good, and
worthie of our imitation: only their longsomeness is wofull at this
time, when their Church Kingdome lyes under a most lamentable
anarchy and confusion.[28]

The historical character of the Assembly is also indicated in
the debates on and resolution of theological issues. Sometimes
the conclusions of these difficult and close debates have been
regarded, by those who have forgotten the historical character of
all assemblies, as a final and almost infallible word. This is nowhere better illustrated than in the debate on the form of baptism. For this reason Lightfoot's account of this debate follows in
full:

> Then fell we upon the work of the day, forward upon the Direc-
> tory for baptism. And the first thing done was, that some reasons
> why baptism should be administered in public, were, upon vote,
> waved in this place.
>
> Mr. *Calamy* moved; That we should express something that bap-
> tism should be as near as possible on the sabbath or lecture-days.
> This was well liked of, and cost a large debate for the framing of it
> up: and here I went out of the Assembly to go to Munden.
>
> *Monday, July* 15.]—This day and this week I was absent from the
> Assembly; because that Thursday was the day of thanksgiving for
> the routing of Prince *Rupert* at York. The work of the Assembly was,
> that they went on in the Directory for baptism.

Monday, July 22.]—This day I was come to town again; and when I came, I found that the Assembly had met this morning, and adjourned themselves till Wednesday fortnight; having now sitten a twelvemonth, and never adjourned of all the time.

Wednesday, Aug. 7.]—This morning we met again; and the first thing done was, a debate about some ministers to be examined, and about some that, having passed the Assembly, prove Anabaptists, and Antinomians; and divers stories were told about the behaviour of some Antinomian preachers: whereupon a committee was chosen to draw up a petition to represent this to the Houses.

Then fell we upon the work of the day; which was, about baptizing "of the child, whether to dip him or sprinkle." And this proposition, "It is lawful and sufficient to besprinkle the child," had been canvassed before our adjourning, and was ready now to vote: but I spake against it, as being very unfit to vote, that it is lawful to sprinkle, when every one grants it. Whereupon, it was fallen upon, sprinkling being granted, whether dipping should be tolerated with it. And here fell we upon a large and long discourse, whether dipping were essential or used in the first institution, or in the Jews' custom. Mr. *Coleman* went about, in a large discourse, to prove טבילה to be dipping over-head. Which I answered at large:—as, 1. Aben Ezra, on Gen. xxxv. says, the Sichemites were admitted to Jacob's house by טבילה: and yet there was no water there, but only Jacob's well: 2. R. Sol. on Exod. xxiv. saith that Israel was entered into covenant with sprinkling of blood and טבילה: which Paul, Heb. ix. expounds of sprinkling of water. 3. That John the Baptist sometimes preached and baptized in places, where he could not possibly dip the parties baptized. This was backed by divers; and it cost a long discourse to prove it: and, in conclusion, I proposed this to the Assembly,—to find in all the Old Testament where "baptizare," when it is used "de sacris," and in "actu transeunte," is not used of sprinkling. It is said, indeed, that the priests washed their bodies, and the unclean washed himself in water, but this was not "actio transiens."

After a long dispute, it was at last put to the question, whether the Directory should run thus,—"The minister shall take water, and sprinkle or pour it with his hand upon the face or forehead of the child:" and it was voted so indifferently, that we were glad to count names twice: for so many were unwilling to have dipping excluded, that the votes came to an equality within one; for the one side was twenty-four,—the other, twenty-five: the twenty-four for the reserving of dipping, and the twenty-five against it: and there grew a great heat upon it: and when we had done all, we concluded upon nothing in it; but the business was recommitted.

Then were produced some letters, sent us out of Holland; first, from Mr. *Strickland,* and then from a synod at Hague: these being read, we adjourned.

Thursday, Aug. 8]—Our first work to-day was, that Dr. *Hoyle* reported the names of three that had been examined for fellowship in Cambridge.

Then fell we upon our work about dipping in baptism: and first it was proposed by Dr. *Burgess,* that our question proposed yesterday might be proposed again. And this cost some time before we could get off this business: at last it was put to the question, Whether the question put yesterday should be more debated before determined; and it was voted affirmatively.

And so we fell upon the business: and I first proposed, that those that stand for dipping, should shew some probable reason, why they hold it. Dr. *Temple* backed me in the thing: and Mr. *Marshal* began; and he said, that he doubted not that all the Assembly concluded that dipping was lawful. I flatly answered, that I hold it unlawful, but an ἐθελο–θζη σκεια; and therefore desired, that it might be proved. But it was first thought fit to go to the business by degrees; and so it was first put to the vote, and voted thus affirmatively,—"that pouring on of water, or sprinkling of it in the administration of baptism, is lawful and sufficient." But I excepted at the word "lawful" as too poor, for that it was as if we should put this query,— Whether it be lawful to administer the Lord's supper in bread and wine? and I moved, that it might be expressed thus,—"It is not only lawful, but also sufficient;" and it was done so accordingly. But as for the dispute itself about dipping, it was thought fit and most safe to let it alone, and to express it thus in our Directory,—"He is to baptize the child with water, which for the manner of doing is not only lawful, but also sufficient, and most expedient to be by pouring or sprinkling water on the face of the child, without any other ceremony." But this cost a great deal of time about the wording it.

After this we went on in the Directory, which was a prayer after the baptizing of the child.

Mr. *Coleman* moved, That the number of the sprinklings might be fixed; but that was not hearkened to.

The prayer of thanksgiving after baptism cost some debate; but, at last, was passed.[29]

The Westminster Assembly was a human achievement, limited as all man's achievements are by finiteness and sin. Nevertheless, the Assembly gave to the world six documents that have contributed to human well-being and to the well-being of the church.

The Confession of Faith
The Larger Catechism
The Shorter Catechism
The Directory for the Public Worship of God
The Form of Presbyterial Church-Government
The Psalter (Rous)

PART II
THE CHARACTER
OF THE CONFESSION

THE WRITING OF THE CONFESSION

The Assembly met on July 1, 1643, and immediately began work on the revision of the Thirty-Nine Articles.[1] Fifteen Articles had been revised by October, but this work was brought to an end by the signing of the Solemn League and Covenant which gave the Assembly new tasks.

The Solemn League and Covenant is a most remarkable document. The English Parliament was concerned for the reformation of the church and had this point of contact with the Scots, but it would have liked a military alliance to unite Scotland and Parliament against the forces of the King. Robert Baillie puts it sharply, "The English were for a civil League, we for a religious Covenant."[2] The Solemn League and Covenant, in original form drafted largely by Alexander Henderson and Johnston of Warriston, reflects the conviction that the unity of a society inheres in its religion and church.[3] A pluralistic, secular society such as ours has difficulty conceiving the unifying force of religion in society and the Solemn League and Covenant as a political document. The Solemn League and Covenant committed the signers to three purposes: (1) to "endeavour the extirpation of Popery, prelacy, . . . superstition, heresy, . . . profaneness; . . ." (2) to "endeavour the preservation of the reformed religion in Scotland, . . ." and "the reformation of religion in the kingdoms of England and Ireland, in doctrine, worship, discipline and government, according to the Word of God and the example of the best reformed Churches;" (3) and to "endeavour to bring the Churches of God in the three kingdoms to the nearest conjunction and uniformity in religion, confession of faith, form of Church government, directory for worship and catechising, that we, and our posterity after us, may, as brethren, live in faith and love, and the Lord may delight to dwell in the midst of us."[4]

Once the Solemn League and Covenant was adopted, the program of the Assembly was both changed and set for the future. The Assembly would have to turn first of all to the form of church government which was not only a critical necessity for a unified society but was also the issue on which the Assembly was most divided. A Directory of Worship supplying guidelines for worship, to replace the *Book of Common Prayer* with its set forms, was prepared at the same time and was completed before the issues of government and discipline were settled because of greater agreement in matters of worship. Only when these tasks were well along would the Assembly turn its attention to a statement of Christian faith.

A committee had been appointed to begin work on the Confession on August 20, 1644; it was composed of Gouge, Gataker, Arrowsmith, Temple, Burroughes, Burges, Vines, Goodwin, and Hoyle. Ten additional members, Palmer, Newcomen, Herle, Reynolds, Wilson, Tuckney, Smith, Young, Ley, and Sedgwicke, were added to the committee on September 4 at the suggestion of the chairman, Dr. Temple.[5] Nothing apparently was done about a confession, however, until in April 1645, when debate about the degree of ignorance or scandal that justified the exclusion of a person from the sacrament laid bare the need for a confession.[6] The Scots also were pressing for the completion of the work of the Assembly.[7] Consequently the House of Commons on April 17, 1645, directed the Assembly to proceed with a confession of faith.[8] It is impossible to reconstruct exactly what happened next. Some apparently wanted a revision of the Thirty-Nine Articles.[9] In any case the decision was made to proceed with a new confession, and a committee composed of Gataker, Harris, Temple, Burges, Reynolds, Hoyle, and Herle was assigned the task of composing a draft of the confession.[10] On July 7 the committee submitted the section on the Scriptures to the Assembly for debate, a debate which continued at least until July 18.[11] On this date Temple presented the statement of the drafting committee concerning God.[12] In the meantime the Assembly decided to divide the work of writing the confession among three committees. The heads of doctrine which had been prepared by the drafting committee were distributed as follows:

On July 16: The first committee: the heads of God and the Holy Trinity, God's decrees, predestination, election, etc., the works of creation and providence, and man's fall. The second committee: sin and the punishment thereof, free will, the covenant of grace, Christ our Mediator. The third committee: effectual vocation, justification, adoption, sanctification.[13]

On November 18: To the first committee: perseverance, Christian liberty, the church, the Communion of Saints. To the second committee: officers and censures of the church, councils or synods, sacraments, baptism, and the Lord's Supper. To the third committee: the law, religion, worship.[14]

On February 23: To the first committee: Christian Sabbath, the civil magistrate, marriage and divorce. To the second committee: certainty of salvation, lies and equivocation, the state of the soul after death. To the third committee: the resurrection, the last judgment, life eternal.[15]

This committee procedure was apparently only a general mode of operation. Sometimes sections were presented by men who were not members of committees to which the topic had been assigned or who were members of no committee.[16] The Assembly also appointed another committee for the rewording and perfecting of the Confession after it had been debated by the Assembly.[17] This committee reported its work back to the Assembly for approval. The care that the Assembly exhibited in its preparation of the Confession justifies the judgment of B. B. Warfield: "The consideration given in the Assembly itself to the several heads was very careful and the scrutiny of every clause and word searching. Recommitments, ordinarily at least to special Committees, were frequent: final dissent on the part of individuals was sometimes entered. In a word, time, pains, and scrupulous care were not spared for perfecting the instrument."[18]

On September 25,1646, more than a year after serious work began on the Confession, the Assembly resolved to send up to the House of Commons the first nineteen chapters of the Confession with the title "to the Honorable the House of Commons assembled in Parliament, The humble advice of the Assembly of Divines, now by authority of Parliament sitting at Westminster, concerning part of a Confession of Faith."[19] The remainder of the Confession was finished by November 26 and sent to Parliament.[20] Parliament, however, requested Scripture proof texts, and this work was not completed until April of 1647.[21] The Assembly had misgivings about the Scripture proofs; they felt that full proof to so large a Confession would require a whole volume. Nevertheless, they went about the task of adding Scripture proofs with the same care with which they wrote the Confession; they checked and rechecked the work of committees and of the Assembly as a whole.[22]

Parliament did not complete its review of the Confession until June of 1648. The title was changed by the House of Commons from Confession of Faith to Articles of Christian Religion, since it was not written in the "I confess" format.[23] The version that was ordered printed by the House of Commons on June 20, 1648, omits Chapter XXX, "Of Church Censures," and Chapter XXXI, "Of Synods and Councils." It also omits the fourth paragraph of Chapter XX which related Christian liberty to the power of the civil magistrate, and part of the fourth paragraph and all of the fifth and sixth paragraphs of Chapter XXIV that have to do with marriage.[24] While Parliament shared the basic theological convictions of the Confession, it is apparent there was no consensus as to the nature of the church or as to the interrelationship of church and society.

In 1654 there was a movement in Cromwell's first Parliament for the calling of a new assembly and the writing of another statement of faith.[25] This came to naught. In 1660 the reassembled Rump Parliament adopted the Confession of the Westminster Assembly with the exception of Chapters XXX and XXXI.[26] This concluded the work that began with hope and expectancy in 1642 and 1643.

In the meantime the Confession had been approved by the General Assembly of the Church of Scotland in 1647, but only after specifying its own interpretation of Chapter XXXI, paragraph 3, that gave the state the right to call synods. The General

Assembly said this would hold only in the case of churches that were not settled or fully constituted.[27] The Parliament of Scotland ratified it in 1649.[28]

The Confession was the work of an English assembly and the commissioners from Scotland. It was a fair summary of the theological consensus among British Protestants, but it never played a significant role in the future of English Protestantism. The Confession was tied to the fate of the Form of Presbyterial Church-Government and the Directory for the Public Worship of God that the Assembly adopted under the strong influence of the Scottish commissioners. Much of the Assembly's work was not acceptable to the Episcopalians on the one hand or the Independents on the other. There was greater unanimity about the Confession, but in the end it also had no enduring influence in the Church of England. Its role was limited to the dissenting churches in England and to the Church of Scotland.

Many reasons can be given for the failure of the Westminster Assembly to shape the future of the Christian community in England. Certainly one of the most important is the difference between the Christian experience in Reformation and post-Reformation Scotland and that in England. William Haller writes:

The Scottish commissioners came to Westminster speaking what seemed the same language but, as we have seen, with meaning drawn from a very different national experience. Their conception of the church did not, at first thought at any rate, appear essentially different from that which had recently been set forth by Smectymnuus, Milton, and other assailants of prelacy. But unlike the English, Scottish reformers had worked out their ideas in the course of a long struggle in an unstable society with a regime at once more arbitrary and less secure. They had contended for nearly a hundred years not simply for freedom to preach but for control of the church itself and through the church for freedom to impose discipline and unity upon a whole nation. English Puritans, though there was no telling how many or with what reservations, might agree in principle that the church was to be acknowledged as an independent kingdom of the spirit in which sovereignty had been vested by Christ in his people and to which civil rulers like other men were subject. Scottish Presbyterians, however, had actually worked out a system of government and discipline embodying this principle, and recent Scottish history was filled with the ups and downs of their endeavor to put the system into effect.[29]

Religious pluralism was now a fact of English life, and in the developing political situation different "denominations" or "sects" acquired sufficient power to protect themselves in some measure. Out of this situation there would develop the modern concept of "denomination" and the acceptance of religious pluralism and tolerance.[30] Furthermore, although Parliament had put down the bishops in Scotland, it was unwilling to erect some new independent church organization that might defy Parliament itself. Neither national experience nor the developing political events, neither the rise of Cromwell nor the later restoration of Charles II favored the Presbyterians or the work of the Westminster Assembly. For this reason the historians have paid little attention to the Assembly and its work. The Scots, however, would adopt the documents of the Assembly and, along with some dissenting groups in England, they would disseminate them throughout the English-speaking world. In the end, the work of the Assembly did become a significant fact in history, though it failed in its English mission.

THE THEOLOGICAL METHOD: MODIFIED SCHOLASTICISM

Theological method is in part determined by the context in which theology is done—by its place in history. Certainly this is true of the Westminster Confession. The Protestant Reformation was a great renewal of faith, and its theology was written out of the immediacy of experience and enthusiasm. This initial period would last for about fifty years. Luther had posted his ninety-five theses on the church door on October 31, 1517, and he had published his great tracts embodying the heart of his theology in 1520. John Calvin had published the first edition of the *Institutes of the Christian Religion* in 1536 and the final edition in 1559. Many of the early Reformed statements of faith had been brief theses, direct and filled with the vitality of public and crucial issues.[1] Even the longer statements had been fragmentary, dealing with the issues immediately in conflict. By 1559 more comprehensive statements of faith which attempted to give a complete statement of Christian belief had begun to appear.[2] In sum, by the seventh decade of the sixteenth century, the critical issues of Protestant faith had been fought through.

After the 1560's Protestant theology faced a new task, namely one of consolidation, clarification, and elaboration. The necessity of this task arose out of the nature of theology itself. During the initial religious experience, words may be used loosely and without careful definition, but if a movement is to survive, it must sooner or later formulate precisely what it is saying or believing. It must ask how one affirmation fits with other affirmations, how the total experience holds together. There are dangers in this process, for when any great experience of life is analyzed, precisely defined, and described, there is the risk that the living reality will be destroyed. But in many areas of life, as psychology demonstrates, this process is necessary for the sake of the health of living experience itself. The new task that theology faced after 1560 was inevitable and ought not to be judged as good or bad in itself, but as a necessary stage in the development of any community or theology.[3]

There were also external forces that contributed to this new theological task. Roman Catholicism, and in particular the Council of Trent (1545–1563), forced Protestant theology to give greater care to the technical aspects of theology. The canons and decrees of the Council were framed not only over against the Protestants but also over against many other expressions of Christian faith that had been live options in medieval Catholicism. The Council provided Roman Catholicism with theological definitions that were relatively clear, precise, and exact. Protestants were therefore required to state their positions more clearly. A comparison of the chapter on justification in the Westminster Confession with Reformed confessions prior to Trent indicates this concern to deal more specifically with the issues involved. Westminster theologians who personally disliked scholastic methods found that they had to make use of those methods in order to deal with their theological opponents.[4] The theological debates that developed between the Reformed and the Lutherans, and that became acrimonious and intense from the 1560's on, likewise led to a fastidious refinement of theological definitions and positions.[5]

The Reformed confessions and theologies of the seventeenth century reflect the changed stance. The Canons of Dort, the Westminster Confession, and the Helvetic Consensus Formula are abstract, objective, and logical in contrast to the historical, experiential, and fragmentary character of the Scots Confession of 1560, the First Helvetic Confession of 1536, and the Genevan Confession of 1536. The seventeenth-century confessions are increasingly more concerned with the authority of faith than with the fact of faith, with the right definition of faith than with proclamation. The Helvetic Consensus Formula goes so far as to claim inspiration for the Hebrew vowel points.[6]

The theological climate of the last fifty years has made it easy to lampoon and to disparage the theology of the seventeenth century. The vibrance and excitement of Luther's theology of the 1520's may well be preferred to the theology of 1620, but history gives no evidence that it is possible to live continually in ecstasy and discovery. Neither is there evidence that the personal and existential can long exist without arousing countermovements or pressures that demand analysis, definition, and systemization. The theological task of the seventeenth century is just as important in its own place as the theology of the first half of the sixteenth century. Twentieth-century theologians as diverse as Karl Barth and Paul Tillich have both expressed their admiration for the technical quality of the theology of the seventeenth century.[7] Robert P. Scharlemann, in a study of the seventeenth-century Lutheran theologian John Gerhard, has written concerning this theology, "There was an intelligible development, motivated by intrinsic as well as extrinsic concerns, and it brought to full expression the theological motifs enunciated by the early Reformers. Its limitations were limitations already present, if only latent, in the sixteenth century; its greatness was due to the same quality as that of Reformation theology—the conception of *fides*."[8] These same words apply to the Westminster Confession, especially when it is read in the context of the sermons that its authors preached.

This development in theology has been called Protestant scholasticism, and its similarity to medieval scholasticism has frequently been noted. Protestant scholasticism, however, is always qualified by the Protestant doctrines of Holy Scripture and justification by faith, which however modified by seventeenth-century developments, also modify the method. Scholasticism is an impossible term to define, for it represents a stance or a perspective as much as a specific procedure. Professor Brian Armstrong has defined scholasticism by referring to four more or less identifiable tendencies.

(1) Primarily it will have reference to that theological approach which asserts religious truth on the basis of deductive ratiocination from given assumptions or principles, thus producing a logically coherent and defensible system of belief. Generally this takes the form of syllogistic reasoning. It is an orientation, it seems, invariably based upon an Aristotelian philosophical commitment and so relates to medieval scholasticism. (2) The term will refer to the employment of reason in religious matters, so that reason assumes at least equal standing with faith in theology, thus jettisoning some of

the authority of revelation. (3) It will comprehend the sentiment that the scriptural record contains a unified, rationally comprehensible account and thus may be formed into a definitive statement which may be used as a measuring stick to determine one's orthodoxy. (4) It will comprehend a pronounced interest in metaphysical matters, in abstract, speculative thought, particularly with reference to the doctrine of God. This distinctive scholastic Protestant position is made to rest on a speculative formulation of the will of God.[9]

On the basis of Armstrong's definition, the Westminster Confession represents a modified scholasticism. The Confession only partially qualifies as a system deduced from any one doctrine or principle. While deductive method was no doubt involved in the Assembly's acceptance of the procedure of "necessary consequence," and while sections of the Confession are developments of a theological principle, the Confession as a whole is certainly not deduced from any one or two principles or doctrines. There are at least four major movements, emphases, or themes in the Confession: the Holy Scripture, the lordship and sovereignty of God, the covenant, and the Christian life. These emphases fit together, but they fit together not so much as a logical system but as character traits fit together in a living person.

The authors of the Confession had a very high regard for human reason, and they certainly intended for their theology to be reasonable. But they never intended for reason to have an equal place with Scripture. When reason did become a source of theology, as it surely did even in the Confession, this was a peril of their theological method, not an intention. Moreover, the use of reason in theology was tempered by the logic of Peter Ramus. Ramus had tied reason to experience. He had used it to analyze and to simplify, not to elaborate speculative theories.

The Westminster theologians did believe that the world and human experience were rational and that the meaning of life could be stated in a comprehensive and precise confession. They did ascribe attributes to God that had been best formulated by medieval scholasticism, but there was no pronounced interest in speculative metaphysical matters. Even the decrees of God were stated with modesty. The authors of the Confession had no doubt that theology was a practical, not a theoretical science, and that the end of life was not the vision of God but a life conformed to his will. Only in a modified sense is the Westminster Confession scholastic.

Our task now is to look more closely at the character of the Confession's theology to note its strengths and its weaknesses. The Confession embodies a theology that attempts to state the Christian faith in precise, abstract propositions that are bound together by impeccable logic. The authors of the Confession had found that logic had a high value. As teachers in pulpits and classrooms, they had discovered that precision and logic were aids in teaching as well as in the solution of theological problems. William Ames wrote in the preface of his theology: "There will be some who condemn the precision of method and logical form as curious and troublesome. But we wish them sounder reason, for they separate the art of learning, judging, and memorizing from those things which most deserve to be learned, known, and memorized."[10] Theology was never an end in itself for the Westminster theologians who were teachers and preachers. The attention given to methods that would aid communication, comprehension, and memory played a significant role in the pervasive influence of Reformed theology in the society of seventeenth-century Britain. The same concern for "method" was evident on the continent, as illustrated in Wollebius' *Compendium.*

Logic was also used as an instrument for laying open a text and for solving a theological problem. William Temple published *A logicall analysis of twentie select psalmes* in 1605. An illustration of his method follows:

> For so we are to apprehend of the Prophets intention in this Psalm, as if in direct terms he reasoned with us thus:
>> If the godly man only be blessed, then in case we desire to be blessed, we ought to betake ourselves to a course of piety.
>> But the godly man only is blessed.
>> Therefore in case we desire to be blessed, we ought to betake ourselves to a course of piety.
> The proposition or first sentence is a particular consequent of a

principle in common reason: namely, That in case we would be possessed of a thing, we must be made capable thereof, and use the means tending thereto. The assumption or second sentence is the question and subject of this whole first Psalm. The conclusion or last sentence is the body and substance of the Psalms following . . .[11]

Another illustration of the method is found in William Ames' *Concerning Conscience:*

The Major of Syllogism, wherein the whole judgement of conscience is laid open, treateth always of the Law, the Minor of the fact and state; and the conclusion of the relation that ariseth from our fact or state, by reason of that Law: which is either guilt, or spiritual joy.

For example,   He that liveth in sin, shall die.
                           Ye live in sin;
                           Therefore ye shall die.

Or thus,   Whoever believeth in Christ, shall not die,
                           But I believe in Christ
Therefore I shall not die, but live. Rom. 8.13.33.34. 1 Joh. 3.19.20.

Conscience in regard of the Major is called Law, in regard of the Minor and conclusion, a Witness; but in regard of the Minor, most properly, an Index, or Book; and in regard of the conclusion, most properly, a Judge. Rom. 2. 14. 15 Rev. 20.12 1 Joh. 5. 10[12]

These illustrations, which can be duplicated over and over again, show how logic becomes a tool of analysis for laying bare the reality of a text or the reality of human existence. But logic can also be the instrument for the elaboration of a theological truth or a Biblical precedent. This logical elaboration, as is indicated elsewhere,[13] is a necessary task of theology, but it is also a tool that allows the mind to develop theological propositions that have no reference to reality. Theology may be impeccable logically but may correspond with nothing in the Holy Scripture or in human experience. Such a theology can continue to exist only as its affirmations become a work of righteousness or merit whereby men are saved by asserting a dead faith, just as they once believed they were saved by a pilgrimage or climbing a stairstep.

For this reason theology must be continually checked by Scripture and experience.

The desire for precise and exact theological definitions caused the Westminster theologians to give up history and imagery drawn from life as tools for writing theology. Theological convictions can be expressed in terms of history, as in much of the Bible, or in terms of abstract propositions. The doctrine of providence can be articulated in the story of Joseph or in the abstract propositions of Chapter V of the Confession. Some of the early Protestant confessions, the Scots Confession of 1560 for example, used Biblical history as the framework on which to hang a great deal of Christian doctrine. This way of writing theology has its advantages. It is easily related to life, and it stimulates the human imagination. It also has its disadvantages; it lacks precision and conciseness; it is open-ended and loose ended. The Westminster theologians preferred an exact theology. This required abstract words and logical formulations. An abstract word leaves no more to the play of imagination than does a mathematical symbol. For this reason the Westminster theologians apparently rejected the Apostles' Creed as the basis for the doctrinal portion of the Shorter Catechism. The Westminster theological method requires a highly disciplined community both in regard to theological knowledge and in regard to life, as can be seen when anyone puts the story of Joseph beside the chapter on providence in the Confession.

An excellent illustration of the way in which the demands of logic take precedence over the experiences of faith is found in a comparison of the treatment of predestination in Calvin's *Institutes* and in the Confession. After much experimentation, Calvin discusses predestination at the conclusion of the Christian life. This was not the logical position, but it was the position that Calvin believed enabled one to best understand the doctrine as a testimony to what God had done in the Christian life. The authors of the Westminster Confession give predestination its more logical place in the third chapter after the chapter on God but before the chapter on creation.

The meticulous care for propositions, precision, and logic

that characterized the work of the Assembly has its unquestioned merit, especially for utility in teaching and in debate with the carefully written theology of the Council of Trent. It also has its perils since it tempts men to think that they have not only life but God under control and to think that they know too much. Once during the Assembly, Thomas Goodwin exclaimed, "Christ did not die for propositions but for persons . . ."[14]

The methodology of the Westminster Assembly was based upon certain implicit assumptions that have to be challenged. One was the assumption that Christian faith can be adequately embodied in propositions. Such an assumption cannot take the incarnation seriously. God's definitive revelation did not come in a proposition but in a person. The fact of the incarnation means that all propositional theology at best approximates the truth. A second assumption is that human reason, either as it exists in men or as it is redeemed by the Holy Spirit, can take the infallible materials of the Bible and radically abstract them into precise propositions, putting them together in a system of impeccable logic. A third assumption is that truth is more adequately expressed in dogmatic pronouncements than in the dialectical tension of opposing views. As the first proposition contradicts the doctrine of the incarnation, so the last two contradict the doctrines of the creatureliness and the sinfulness of man.

It is interesting to note that while the Assembly was sitting, John Milton was writing his *Areopagitica*. In this work he expounds a different understanding of man's grasp of truth:

> A man may be a heretick in the truth; and if he beleeve things only because his Pastor sayes so, or the Assembly so determins, without knowing other reason, though his belief be true, yet the very truth he holds, becomes his heresie. There is not any burden that som would gladlier post off to another, then the charge and care of their Religion. There be, who knows not that there be of Protestants and professors who live and dye in as arrant an implicit faith, as any lay Papist of Loretto. A wealthy man addicted to his pleasure and to his profits, finds Religion to be a traffick so entangl'd, and of so many piddling accounts, that of all mysteries he cannot skill to keep a stock going upon that trade. What should he doe? fain he would have the name to be religious, fain he would bear up with his

neighbours in that. What does he therefore, but resolve to give over toyling, and to find himself out som factor, to whose care and credit he may commit the whole managing of his religious affairs; som Divine of note and estimation that must be. To him he adheres, resigns the whole ware-house of his religion, with all the locks and keyes into his custody; and indeed makes the very person of that man his religion; esteems his associating with him a sufficient evidence and commendatory of his own piety.

. . . . .

To be still searching what we know not, by what we know, still closing up truth to truth as we find it (for all her body is *homogeneal,* and proportionall) this is the golden rule in *Theology* as well as in Arithmetick, and makes up the best harmony in a Church; not the forc't and outward union of cold, and neutrall, and inwardly divided minds.

. . . . .

And though all the windes of doctrin were let loose to play upon the earth, so Truth be in the field, we do injuriously by licensing and prohibiting to misdoubt her strength. Let her and Falshood grapple; who ever knew Truth put to the wors, in a free and open encounter. Her confuting is the best and surest suppressing. He who hears what praying there is for light and clearer knowledge to be sent down among us, would think of other matters to be constituted beyond the discipline of *Geneva,* fram'd and fabric't already to our hands.

For who knows not that Truth is strong next to the Almighty; she needs no policies, nor stratagems, nor licencings to make her victorious, those are the shifts and the defences that error uses against her power: give her but room, and do not bind her when she sleeps, for then she speaks not true, as the old *Proteus* did, who spake oracles only when he was caught and bound, but then rather she turns herself into all shapes, except her own, and perhaps tunes her voice according to the time, as *Micaiah* did before *Ahab,* untill she be adjur'd into her own likenes. Yet it is not impossible that she may have more shapes than one. What else is all that rank of things indifferent, wherein Truth may be on this side, or on the other, without being unlike her self.[15]

Milton was unduly optimistic about the power of truth, as events of the past half-century have indicated. He was, at the same time, closer to the Calvinist doctrine of man and his power to *know* the truth than were his contemporaries in the Assembly.

As Reinhold Niebuhr has put it, it is impossible for man to know
the truth, and it is impossible for him to keep from pretending
that he does.[16] This pretense may be the ultimate sin in theology.

Milton's "On the Forcers of Conscience" was written in the
heat of controversy with the Assembly, but it should be a warning
to all theologians:

> Because you have thrown off your Prelate lord,
>   And with stiff vows renounced his Liturgy,
>   To seize the widowed whore Plurality
>   From them whose sin ye envied, not abhorred,
> Dare ye for this adjure the civil sword
>   To force our consciences that Christ set free,
>   And ride us with a Classic Hierarchy,
>   Taught ye by mere *A.S.* and *Rutherford?*
> Men whose life, learning, faith, and pure intent
>   Would have been held in high esteem with Paul,
>   Must now be named and printed heretics
> By *shallow Edwards* and *Scotch What d'ye call.*
>   But we do hope to find out all your tricks,
>   Your plots and packing, worse than those of Trent,
>   That so the Parliament
> May, with their wholesome and preventive shears,
> Clip your phylacteries, though baulk your ears,
>   And succour our just fears,
> When they shall read this clearly in your charge—
> NEW PRESBYTER is but old PRIEST writ large.[17]

The theological methodology of the Westminster documents is only *one* of the ways in which the Reformed community
worked out its theology. The contrast is most clearly seen in the
Scots Confession of 1560. The Scots Confession used the framework of history—God's dealing with his people from Adam to
Christ, and the decisive events in the life of Jesus Christ—as the
framework of its theology. The consequence is that the doctrinal
affirmations of the Scots Confession lack the precision, finality,
and completeness of those of the Westminster Confession. It is
not clear, however, that the Scots Confession is inferior in point-
ing men to God or in serving as man's confession of his faith.

THE BIBLE

The Assembly apparently had no difficulty deciding how the Confession should begin. The Reformed tradition favored, though not unanimously, an opening chapter on the Holy Scripture.[1] This starting point came naturally to the Puritans whose own experience was deeply rooted in and oriented by the Bible. They wanted to begin the Catechisms, however, with a different question, "What is the chief and highest end of man?" They then proceeded to the Word of God, the only rule of faith and obedience. The men of the Assembly were bound by a rule of Parliament that every statement had to be rooted in the Bible.[2] But this was a rule they would have observed anyway.

The chapter "Of the Holy Scripture," in literary expression and in theological excellence, is worthy of its place in the Confession. It is as fine an example of confessional writing as is to be found anywhere in the Christian tradition. "There is certainly," writes B. B. Warfield, "in the whole mass of confessional literature no more nobly conceived or ably wrought-out statement of doctrine than the chapter 'Of the Holy Scripture,' which the Westminster Divines placed at the head of their Confession and laid at the foundation of their system of doctrine."[3] Warfield was committed to the Westminster doctrine, but even those who differ with the doctrine have to admire the theological brilliance. The thought is clearly expressed in chaste, precise language. Two words are never used where one word, rightly chosen, will do. Each word fits and carries its load of freight. The authors wanted each statement to correspond with reality. They cut away the dubious and did not overstate their beliefs. The thought is clearly formulated. The argument of the chapter runs smoothly in a coherent pattern. Consequently, this chapter has stood the tests of time remarkably well. This is surprising in as much as the revolution in historical methods and thinking has changed the way men understand the Bible as much or more than has been the case with any article in the creed. Extraneous material, such as the authorship of certain books of the Bible or a theology of

inspiration, which modern scholarship has discredited, was omitted. In simple, unadorned words the Westminster theologians
expressed the hard substance of their faith that the Holy Scripture is the place where God speaks to man. The result is that a
modern man, who uses the tools of critical study but who has the
faith that God does reveal himself in Scripture, can affirm this
formulation of men who were not confronted by our modern
problems.

"Of the Holy Scripture" is an introduction to the theology
of the Confession in as much as it lays out the sources of theology
and suggests how the theologian moves from the sources to his
theological confession, that is, to what he has to say in his own
time on the basis of what is said in the Bible. The authors of the
Confession were sure that God had revealed himself through the
"light of nature." By "light of nature" the members of the Assembly meant, according to the studies of Jack Bartlett Rogers,
"a direct revelation of God implanted in the heart of man, a *sensus
divinitatis,* which remains, by God's common grace, even after the
Fall, though defaced and dimmed."[4] They were also sure that
God revealed himself through his works of creation and through
providence. They did not denigrate this revelation. It was enough
to leave man without excuse, but it was not sufficient for man's
salvation. Therefore, the Holy Scriptures are indispensable.
They are "the word of God written," "the rule of faith and life,"
"infallible truth and divine authority," and the "Supreme Judge
by which all controversies of religion are to be determined, and
can be no other but the Holy Spirit speaking . . ." (The Confession I)* The theological problem inheres in the difficulty in mov-
ing from the Word of Scripture to what the Christian must say
in his own time. Theology is not the simple repetition of the
Bible, but speaking about God and man today on the basis of the
Holy Scripture.

There is no question that the authors of the Confession

---

*All quotations marked The Confession are taken from a critical text of the
Confession in S. W. Carruthers, *The Westminster Confession of Faith* (Manchester: R.
Aikman & Son, 1937).

believed that the Bible was inspired and that God revealed himself in propositions. In fact, no one with whom the Assembly
dealt seriously denied the inspiration of the Bible. The Assembly
had to deal, rather, with those who did not want to limit inspiration to the Bible.[5] Most of the questions that have developed
about the nature and extent of the inspiration of the Bible have
arisen since the Confession was written. The results of historical
and scientific studies began to make affirmations of the inerrancy
of the Bible on matters of history and science very difficult more
than a century ago. Those who equated the Bible as the revelation of God with inerrancy were faced with the desperate task of
denying that errors were to be found in the Scriptures. One of
the more scholarly examples of this controversy took place in the
1880's between B. B. Warfield and A. A. Hodge, both of Princeton Theological Seminary, arguing for inerrancy, and Charles A.
Briggs of Union Theological Seminary in New York defending a
more liberal position.[6] Each tried to claim the Westminster Confession for his own position. Two excellent results came from the
debate. One benefit of the debate was a series of scholarly studies
of the Westminster Assembly, and the other was the remarkable
accumulation of literature on the Westminster Assembly in the
McAlpin Library of Union Theological Seminary in New York.
The substance of the debate, however, was inconclusive and
unrewarding, for both Warfield and Briggs were attempting to
force the Confession to answer questions the Confession never
faced. The authors of the Confession believed that the Bible was
inspired, and that as a consequence, it was "the rule of faith and
life," and "the infallible truth and divine authority." How they
would have responded if they had been confronted with the
problems raised by critical study today, we can only conjecture.
The Puritans and their theological forefathers had taken the Bible with historical seriousness. They had, since Tyndale and Calvin, insisted upon the historical and the literary or natural meaning of Scripture, but they had had little awareness of the issues
that historical study would eventually raise for theology in general and for the doctrine of Scripture in particular.

It suffices for our purpose to note that the Assembly re-

garded the Bible as the source of infallible truth. Any awareness
of historical, scientific, or grammatical errors made no dint in this
conviction. In part this infallible truth was expressly set down.[7]
In part it could be deduced from Scripture. In the study of Scripture the members of the Assembly made use of "logical analysis,"
and historical and literary criteria. They wanted to find the literary and historical sense of the passage. These tools of study and
understanding, however, were subordinate to their conviction
that the Bible was the Word of God written. The tools of study
had not yet raised questions about the prior conviction.

There is no doubt that the authors of the Confession were
convinced that God's infallible truth was embodied in propositions. The very character of the Westminster Confession as a
seventeenth-century document accentuates this perspective. The
chapter on saving faith could give, as a subordinate definition of
saving faith, believing as true whatsoever is revealed in the Word.
The Reformers of the sixteenth century and the writers of the
Scots Confession of 1560 and the Second Helvetic Confession
likewise believed that God's infallible truth was embodied in
propositions. The emphasis however was different. Faith was not
so much believing that whatever was in the Bible was true; faith
was trust in the God and Father of the Lord Jesus Christ. Many
Puritan sermons, it must be said, had this same character. The
shift in perspective of the Confession, though subtle, was none-
theless real and important. It encouraged the formulation of a
theology in abstract and even legal terms that in many cases were
remote from Christian experience or the work of the Holy Spirit
in the believer. In reaction to this type of theology, Schleiermacher, a century and a half later, would reverse the whole
procedure of theology and define theology as the articulation of
the experience of the Christian community.

The sermons and treatises of members of the Assembly
made great use of the Bible, and the fact that the members were
not modern men must not obscure their skill as interpreters.
Their theology and their sermons were, for the most part, commentary on Scripture. They expressly intended that sermons
should be based on Scripture, that doctrines should be raised

from a block of Scripture, and that the doctrines should be applied in a plain and pertinent manner.[8] It is doubtful if preaching has ever been more effective than the plain-style preaching of the Puritans was. The footnotes to the Confession obscure the manner in which the members of the Assembly wrestled with Scripture according to the best scholarship of their day. They found in sections of Scripture "precedents" from which they could proclaim God's will for their day and in the light of which they could understand their own time. The combination of the profound conviction that the Bible was the Word of God and of techniques by which the Puritans moved from the Bible to the events of their time contributed to their "toughness" of mind and character.

The task of theology, in distinction from that of Biblical study in which one must first understand what the Bible actually says in its own context, is to move from the Holy Scripture to the contemporary situation, to say in the context of present-day experience what must be said by those who believe that the Bible is the revelation of God. For the members of the Assembly this was not as difficult a task as it is for us today. They understood their world very much as the people of the New Testament understood their world. There is a far deeper gulf between the last third of the twentieth century and the world of the Westminster Assembly than there was between the world of the Westminster Assembly and that of the New Testament. This new cultural situation reveals inadequacies in the method by which the writers of the Confession moved from the Holy Scripture to the contemporary situation that were not obvious to wise and able theologians of the seventeenth century.

The Assembly's high doctrine of Scripture made the principle of interpretation, by which the theologian moved from Scripture to theology, of decisive importance. As has been indicated, the members of the Assembly presupposed the use of the canons and rules of logic, history, and grammar in the study of Scripture, though they did not anticipate many of the results of this study. A second hermeneutical principle was the interpretation of Scripture by Scripture: "The infallible rule of interpretation of Scrip-

ture, is the Scripture itself . . ." (The Confession I, 9) The less
clear must be understood in terms of the more clear. Moreover,
the message of the Bible is not a series of discrete and independent affirmations, but a coherent unity. In other words the Bible
is not a series of proof texts, but one message, and individual
texts must be understood in terms of the whole.

This emphasis upon the interpretation of Scripture by Scripture tended, however, to a Biblicism that became increasingly
isolated from life and from the world. Earlier Reformed statements on Biblical interpretation had insisted upon two additional
principles which were omitted in the Westminster documents.
One of these was the analogy of faith or the creed.[9] Scripture
must be interpreted in the light of the Christian community's
understanding of Scripture in the past. The Reformed theologians were always willing to reform the creeds in the light of
Scripture, but they equally insisted that the church's understanding of Scripture was an indispensable aid to understanding Scripture in the present. The Westminster documents minimized the
importance of the analogy of faith. In the end, the interpretation
of Scripture was impoverished by the isolation of the interpreter
from the Christian community.

Reformed hermeneutics also insisted on the rule of love as
a principle of interpretation.[10] The sum of the law is love for God
and love for neighbor. Hence all proper interpretations of Scripture will enhance love, and any interpretation that does not build
up brotherhood must be reexamined. The early Reformed creeds
were all documents with strong ethical thrusts. This is one of
their most distinguishable characteristics. The exposition of the
Ten Commandments in the Westminster Larger Catechism is a
very important ethical treatise. The refutation of Antinomianism
was one of the primary concerns of the Assembly. Nevertheless,
the dropping of the rule of charity as an interpretative principle
had devastating consequences in the future as doctrine would
tend to become divorced from practice.

The dropping of these two classic interpretative guides contributed to the development of a sterile Biblicism. It encouraged
men to believe that, having the Bible, they could dispense with

the wisdom of the Christian community. It encouraged the exal-
tation of right doctrine above right living, though Calvin had
insisted that ethics was the best test of doctrine. Finally, this
method of interpretation encouraged the isolation of theology
from the world of culture in general. The interpreter studied his
Bible alone, dispensing with dialogue with the world.

A third principle of interpretation adopted for the Westminster Confession was that doctrine "by good and necessary consequence may be deduced from Scripture." (The Confession I, 6)
The minutes of the Assembly reveal that "good and necessary
consequence," as a way of getting from the Bible to the contemporary situation, was discussed though it was not debated in
these terms.[11] The question was "How is the will and appointment of Jesus Christ set out in Scripture?" The first answer was
in the express words of Jesus. Certainly in the seventeenth century it was possible to move from the words of Jesus to the
contemporary situation, or so it seemed. Today it is not so simple, as anyone who has tried applying the words of Jesus directly
and without interpretation to contemporary situations knows full
well. The Assembly then ordered that another method by which
the will and appointment of Jesus could be set forth was necessary consequence. The Assembly simply confirmed in debate the
theological method that was widely used by Puritan preachers
and theologians. All theology is in some measure dependent on
this method, as all theologians have known since the time Augustine reflected upon the theological task.[12] The distinguishing
characteristic of the Westminster Assembly was the evident confidence in the power of reason, especially a regenerate reason, to
carry out the theological task.

George Gillespie, a Scottish commissioner to the Assembly,
describes this theological method as follows:

> **Chapter XX. That necessary consequences from the written
> Word of God do sufficiently and strongly prove the conse-
> quent or conclusion, if theoretical, to be a certain divine
> truth which ought to be believed, and, if practical, to be a
> necessary duty which we are obliged unto, jure divino.**

This assertion must neither be so far enlarged as to comprehend the erroneous reasonings and consequences from Scripture which this or that man, or this or that church, apprehend and believe to be strong and necessary consequences (I speak of what *is*, not of what is *thought to be* a necessary consequence): neither yet must it be so far contracted and straitened as the Arminians would have it, who admit of no proofs from Scripture, but either plain explicit texts, or such consequences are *nulli non obviae*, as neither are, nor can be, controverted by any man who is *rationis compos*; . . . by which principle, if embraced, we must renounce many necessary truths which the reformed churches hold against the Arians, Antitrinitarians, Socinians, Papists, because the consequences and arguments from Scripture brought to prove them are not admitted as good by the adversaries.

This also I must, in the second place, premise, that the meaning of the assertion is not that human reason, drawing a consequence from Scripture, can be the ground of our belief or conscience; for although the consequence or argumentation be drawn forth by men's reasons, yet the consequent itself, or conclusion, is not believed nor embraced by the strength of reason, but because it is the truth and will of God, . . .

Thirdly, Let us here observe with Gerhard, a distinction between corrupt reason and renewed or rectified reason; . . . It is the latter, not the former reason, which will be convinced and satisfied with consequences and conclusions drawn from Scripture, in things which concern the glory of God, and matters spiritual or divine.[13]

All Christian theology must move in some such way, as Gillespie describes, from the revelatory event. Every theological movement, however, must be modest and rigorously criticized. Otherwise, theology may become human fantasy. It must be checked always by its Biblical reference and by its correspondence to the facts of experience.

In sum, Biblical interpretation, as practiced by the Westminster Assembly, includes the following principles: (1) a high doctrine of Scripture as the Word of God written; (2) the historical and literary study of Scripture, though with no awareness of the issues these methods would raise; (3) the infallible interpreter of Scripture is Scripture; (4) doctrine "by good and necessary consequence" may be deduced from Scripture. It must be noted that in the task of Biblical interpretation, the Confession: (1)

omits faith and charity; (2) neglects the role of Christian experience or the work of the Holy Spirit; (3) isolates theology from any
dialogue with culture. In addition the doctrine of the covenants
did not have the hermeneutical significance at Westminster as in
the more decisively covenant theologies.

The consequences of these hermeneutical principles are
clearly indicated in the subsequent history of the Confession. A
theology that began with the infallible materials of the Bible and
that was developed by a fully competent reason easily became
infallible for practical purposes. Furthermore, since it was no
longer necessary to take seriously either the wisdom of the Christian community or the questions that culture (science, history,
etc.) raised, theology became increasingly obscurantic and isolated. In addition, the failure to relate theology to experience or
to check its speculation with what actually happened in the lives
of Christians led to a theology that was difficult to recognize in
Christian experience.

The inadequacy of the Assembly's understanding of theological method must not obscure the real validity of the Confession. All theology must make use of "necessary consequence" as
one method of doing theology, that is, if it takes the "revelatory
event" seriously and wishes to relate it to a new time and a new
place. What must be learned from Westminster is that when this
procedure is trusted too much, theology tends to say more and
to say it more dogmatically than it properly should. It must also
be learned that theological formulations must always be related
to Christian experience, for when theology describes what the
Christian community does not experience, then that theology is
doomed. Whitehead speaks of the fallacy of misplaced concreteness.[14] The theological method of the Assembly led to misplaced
concreteness in theology, the attributing of concreteness or reality to what is tenuous, or without reference to reality. These
perils, which were latent in the writing of the Confession, would
become critical when the Confession was used by later genera-
tions in new cultural settings.

The authors of the Westminster Confession were theologians of the Bible. Few, if any, have ever excelled them in effective

preaching of the Biblical message. No creedal statement excels the technical quality of the chapter "Of the Holy Scripture." Nevertheless there were hidden flaws which proved destructive, especially when the Confession was simply repeated in a new time and place.

The Lordship and Sovereignty of God

The writers of the Confession had no doubt about the lordship and the sovereignty of God. The light of nature shows forth the lordship and sovereignty of God and the Scriptures abundantly declare it (The Confession XXI, 1). Moreover, the authors of the Confession believed that this conviction had been confirmed in their experience and history. " . . . the Puritan mind," it has been observed, "was one of the toughest the world has ever had to deal with. It is impossible to conceive of a disillusioned Puritan; no matter what misfortune befell him, no matter how often or how tragically his fellowmen failed him, he would have been prepared for the worst, and would have expected no better."[1] Insofar as these words are true of the Puritans, they are rooted in the Puritan's faith in God and in the sovereignty of his decrees, that is, God's purposes in human history.

The lordship and sovereignty of God are repeatedly affirmed in the Confession. When the writers of the Confession attempted to say who God is, they declared their belief in the "one only living and true God . . . working all things according to the counsel of His own immutable and most righteous will . . . " (The Confession II, 1) When they spoke of God's eternal decree, that is, his eternal purpose, they declared that "from all eternity, [he] did by the most wise and holy counsel of his own will, freely, and unchangeably ordain whatsoever comes to pass." (The Confession III, 1) In the chapter on providence they wrote, "God the great Creator of all things doth uphold, direct, dispose, and govern all creatures, actions, and things, from the greatest even to the least, by His most wise and holy providence, according to His infallible fore-knowledge and the free and immutable counsel of His own will . . ." (The Confession V, 1) Chapter X, "Of Effectual Calling," affirms the sovereignty of God in regard to salvation. Those whom God predestines he calls effectually by his word and Spirit. God's sovereignty is not only affirmed over nature and over man and his salvation but also over government. God "hath ordained civil magistrates to be, under Him, over the people, for His own glory, and the public good . . ." (The Confession XXIII, 1)

The Confession's statements of the lordship and sovereignty of God are abstract, but the writers of the Confession had no difficulty relating them to the concrete facts of experience. They had no problem in believing that the natural order was expressive of the divine purposes. Galileo had shifted the attention of men from the "why" of physical events to the "how," that is, to a mathematical formula expressing their purposes and motions.[2] But the scientific developments that were taking place did not seem to bother the theologians, though certainly some of them were fully acquainted with them. Newton would publish his *Principia* in 1687, and in so doing he would undercut the theological conviction that the universe is immediately expressive of the will and purposes of God. The popular picture of the world became that of a machine, like the giant Strasbourg clock, that ran chiefly by its own mechanism. The philosopher of science, E. A. Burtt, has written that " . . . Newton's authority was squarely behind that view of the cosmos which saw in man a puny, irrelevant spectator (so far as a being wholly imprisoned in a dark room can be called such) of the vast mathematical system whose regular motions according to mechanical principles constituted the world of nature. . . . The world that people had thought themselves living in —a world rich with colour and sound, redolent with fragrance, filled with gladness, love and beauty, speaking everywhere of purposive harmony and creative ideals—was crowded now into minute corners in the brains of scattered organic beings. The really important world outside was a world hard, cold, colourless, silent, and dead; a world of quantity, a world of mathematically computable motions in mechanical regularity."[3] The language of the Confession, affirming the purposes of God, made sense in the world view of the writers of the Confession, but it did not make sense in the world that Burtt describes. The problem with the Confession today is not so much that the language is out-of-date or that the intent of the authors is wrong, assuming one takes seriously the portrayal of the nature of God in the Holy Scriptures, but it is the failure or inability of the contemporary theologian to speak meaningfully about the purposive action of God in the natural order.

The lordship of God was dramatically expressed in history for the writers of the Confession. They thought of the Christian life as participation in the dramas of history, and they believed that they were the instruments of the divine purpose. Lord Eustace Percy in his perceptive biography of John Knox wrote that John Calvin in the *Institutes* gave expression to something "much more explosive than the dogma of predestination. [The *Institutes*] contained a philosophy of history, a statement of Christian faith in terms of divine purpose."[4] Calvin did not limit God's sovereignty to the narrow verdict of condemnation or acquittal for the individual soul; he also focused attention on the whole drama of human history. "He could not paint the ultimate destinies of man in milder colours than his contemporaries, but he directed men's eyes to more immediate issues, and gave them, in practice, a nobler incentive to action than the hope of heaven or the fear of hell."[5] God was working his purposes out in human history, and he was calling men to be the instruments of his purpose. The English Reformed theologians believed that England was God's elect nation for the accomplishment of his purposes, and they were about the task of establishing the New Jerusalem "in England's green and pleasant land."[6]

The sense of participating in the drama of world history with the conviction that God's eternal purposes were being worked out in that history is not immediately clear from the abstract language of the Confession. Many have read the Confession and even memorized the Catechisms without being able to turn the abstract vocabulary into the flesh and blood of experience. The writers of the Confession did not have this trouble. Members of the Assembly made use of the practice of sermons before Parliament to proclaim the abstract theology of the Confession in Biblical and concrete images and with concrete historical reference. James Spalding, in a study of these sermons, has likened them to a public diary—the counterpart of the Puritan's private diary—in which the preacher registered his assessment of what God was doing in English and world history.[7] Spalding finds the pattern of these sermons is Deuteronomic, interpreting Israel's history in terms of judgments and blessings based on the examples of Joshua, Judges, First and Second Samuel, and First and Second Kings. The Deuteronomic motif, however, does not cover all the preaching. There is also an apocalyptic element with its "declaration that, appearances to the contrary notwithstanding, God ruled the course of historical events and would bring out of the ominous present a glorious future quite independently of human agency."[8] The abstract and theological language of the Confession is not deadly, dull jargon but a precise and exact statement of the conviction that God is the Lord of nature and history.

The writers of the Confession liked to use the word *decree*. They argued whether it was more proper to speak of God's decree or decrees.[9] Decree is not a word that is easily used today, and for this reason it will help to quote the excellent definition of decree, as it was used in Reformed theology, from Edward D. Morris' commentary on the Confession.

> The term, decree, is here employed to express the generic proposition that *God from all eternity did, by the most wise and holy counsel of his own will, freely and unchangeably ordain whatsoever comes to pass.* Such terms as predestination, foreordination, election, reprobation, preterition, relate to the divine decree as manifested within the particular sphere of grace. In the more generic or comprehensive sense, covering the entire field of the divine activity, the term, decree, has its closest synonyms in such words as plan, design, purpose, scheme, project, ordinance, edict. It is both a thought resident eternally in the divine mind, and an intention to give expression to that thought in correspondent action wrought out in time. It involves both prevision and predetermination—the ability to devise and the ability to execute what is devised in every sphere. It does not imply volition or action without purpose, or a merely arbitrary election without regard to conditions, or activity unregulated by the moral qualities inherent in Deity. It differs radically from the pagan notion of fate, by the cardinal fact that it is personal both in the design and in the execution. It involves a true and proper sovereignty such as a supreme person may exercise, but a holy sovereignty which carries in it not only omnipotence but wisdom and love and righteousness. In substance it implies, in the words of another,

(Smith, H. B. Christ. Theol.) that the present system of the universe in all its parts, as it was and is and is to be, was an eternal plan or purpose in the divine Mind.[10]

John Calvin used the word *decree* only infrequently.[11] Reformed theologians of the last half of the sixteenth century and first half of the seventeenth used it with increasing frequency. As they defined it with increasing precision, subtle differences developed between their theologies and Calvin's. This is illustrated in the fact that Calvin discussed the doctrine of predestination after he had worked through the doctrine of the Christian life and just before the chapter on the resurrection. Westminster treats the decrees in Chapter III after the doctrine of God and before the doctrine of creation. The result is a much tighter system and greater difficulty in dealing adequately with the human response.

The Confession's statement of the sovereignty and the lordship of God is shaped by the native British, Augustinian tradition and by the Arminian controversy as well as by Calvin's theology. Nevertheless, the Westminster emphasis on the lordship and sovereignty of God is at one with the Calvinist tradition in general purpose. The whole Reformed tradition wanted to emphasize that the purposes of God are being worked out in nature and in history and that they will be frustrated by the intractability of neither. No other theological theme is so perennially a task for theology on the part of those who believe that God is the Creator and Redeemer, and no other theme illustrates so well that all theology is written for time, not for eternity.

The Covenant Theology

The most striking innovation in Reformed theology in the seventeenth century was the development of covenant theology. All Christian theology must include some notion of the covenant, for the covenant is an indispensable element in Biblical faith and history. Along with election, covenant is a preeminent expression of God's saving activity among men. God chose Abraham and made a covenant with him. God delivered the children of Israel from Egypt, the land of bondage, and covenanted with them at Sinai. Biblical faith can be reduced to neither election nor covenant. Yet no Biblical faith is adequate without either, and it is therefore to be expected that election and covenant would be motifs in any statement of Christian faith that attempts to be as systematic and comprehensive as Westminster. There are elements of the Biblical message that are not easily included under either motif, and for this reason neither can be made an all-encompassing theological principle.[1]

The role of the covenant in God's dealing with his people was clearly enunciated in early Reformed theology. Calvin devoted three chapters in the *Institutes* to the development of the Covenant of Grace.[2] His emphasis on the covenant is even more pronounced in his sermons and comments on the Scriptures.[3] Nevertheless, the idea of the covenant is not as controlling for Calvin's theology as is the idea of election or the reality and nature of faith. Bullinger, Zwingli's great successor in Zurich, made greater use of the covenant in his exposition of the Christian faith in the *Decades,* a series of fifty sermons that were required reading for English churchmen in the sixteenth century.[4] The real development of covenant theology came in the latter part of the sixteenth century and in the seventeenth century. The role of the covenant or covenants became the framework for articulating the faith. In the end, the faith was stated simply in terms of the covenants.

Covenant theology was elaborated in the form of two covenants. The first was a Covenant of Works or of Nature, made with

Adam. In this covenant God promised salvation to man on condition of perfect obedience and gave to man the power to fulfill the
law. This was not simply a covenant of merit, for the covenant
itself was a gracious act of God, the great disparity between God
and man prohibiting any possibility of man's works by their own
merit earning salvation. The Covenant of Works was broken by
man's disobedience, but it clearly proclaimed that man as man,
no matter how much he may deny it, is tied to God by covenant.
The Scriptual basis for this covenant was meager, but it was
necessary as the background of the Covenant of Grace and to put
the Covenant of Grace in the context of world history.[5]

The whole of Biblical history, with the exception of a portion
of Adam's life and experience, belongs to the Covenant of Grace.
By this covenant, God promises salvation to man not on the basis
of his works, but on the basis of his faith. This covenant found
preeminent expression in the call of Abraham, the deliverance
from Egypt, the giving of the law at Sinai, and above all in the
event of Jesus Christ. The covenant was administered in different
ways in the Old and New Testaments, but it is one Covenant of
Grace that includes both Abraham and Paul.

The development of covenant theology took place, apparently, in considerable independence on the continent and in
Britain. One of the earliest theologians to develop the covenant
theology in Britain was Rollock (1555–1599), an Edinburgh
theologian.[6] The role of the covenant in systematic theology was
further developed by William Perkins, Sibbes, Preston, and William Ames. John Ball's comprehensive statement of Christian
theology, under the rubric of the covenant, *The Covenant of Grace*,
was published while the Assembly was meeting.[7] The role of the
covenant in theology was also being developed on the continent
and received a classic statement in Cocceius' *Summa doctrinae de
Foedere et Testamento Dei* in 1648, the year after the Assembly
concluded most of its theological work.

Covenant theology was incorporated into the standard statements of Reformed theology in the seventeenth century. It had
merited brief mention in the Irish Articles of 1615 and was developed in greater detail in the Westminster Confession and Cate-

chisms. It was also included in that final statement of Reformed scholasticism, the Helvetic Consensus Formula, and in the systematic theology of that impeccably orthodox theologian Turretin of Geneva.

The covenant theology modified Reformed scholasticism in a number of ways. First of all, it directed the attention away from the decrees of God, abstractly considered, to the working out of the divine decrees in history. The contemplation of the divine decrees in abstraction led to dizzy heights of speculation. Concentration upon the actual working out of the decrees focused theology on what God had actually done in history. In the second place, covenant theology tied theological work more closely to the Bible, for the covenants were an important part of Biblical history. It is true that the covenant theologians could find ways for abstract speculation, as in the development of the idea of the covenant between God the Father and God the Son. For the most part, however, covenant theology fastened attention upon history. In the third place, covenant theology provided a rational scheme for interpreting God's ways with man. God was still the Lord, and his ways were still beyond man's comprehension. Yet within a limited sphere, man could decipher the divine purposes and understand human destiny. In the fourth place, covenant theology gave theology a universal scope. The Covenant of Works or Covenant of Life was in some measure speculative, but it did provide the theological means of relating the Christian community to universal history. All men stood under this covenant. Thus it enabled the Christian who stood under the Covenant of Grace to speak in the name of God to the non-Christian who, whether he chose or not, was under the Covenant of Works. Finally, covenant theology made it necessary for the theologian to pay some attention to human response and to the importance of human decision. The initiative in the covenant was always with God, but man's response to this initiative was still a vital factor. Covenant theology was thus a means of recovering an authentic aspect of all Christian experience that a speculative doctrine of the divine decrees was in danger of losing.

The occasion for the development of covenant theology is

readily apparent. Reformed scholasticism had grown increasingly abstract; that is, it increasingly used language that was separated from experience. It increasingly emphasized the decrees of God, rather than the working out of the decrees in Christian experience and history. Abstract language and preoccupation with the decrees of God made theology the enterprise of heroic and disciplined souls. Ordinary people who thought in terms of the concrete actualities of experience were excluded by this theology. Covenant theology allowed the theological enterprise to state the faith in terms of the actual working out of God's purposes in experience and in history.

Chapter VII of the Confession is entitled "Of God's Covenant With Man." It begins with the Covenant of Works. Even though man by creation was obligated to obey his Creator, such obedience would have brought him no blessing because of the great disparity between Creator and creature. God graciously condescended to man's condition and established a Covenant of Works by which man could gain blessedness on the condition of perfect obedience. The moral law which was the condition of this covenant was God's perfect rule of righteousness for man; this law was later delivered by God on Sinai in the Ten Commandments. This covenant was broken by man's sin. God was then pleased to make a second covenant, commonly called the Covenant of Grace. The Confession then goes on to elaborate how this covenant was administered in different ways in Biblical history.

B. B. Warfield contended that "The architectonic principle of the Westminster Confession is supplied by the schematization of the Federal Theology."[8] No one can lightly disagree with Warfield, but the evidence does not seem to support his contention. Covenant theology was one of the organizing movements of the Confession, but certainly it was not the only one or even the dominant one. When one contrasts the Confession with John Ball's statement of Christian faith in terms of the covenants, in a work that was known by the Assembly and in which the whole of Christian faith is expressed in terms of the covenants, it becomes clear that the Confession makes use of covenant theology but is not exclusively covenant theology by any means.

Critics of covenant theology have insisted that the covenants modified the theology of Calvin. Perry Miller in his studies of Puritanism concludes that covenant theology was "simply an idiom in which these Protestants sought to make a bit more plausible the mysteries of the Protestant creed."[9] Yet in so doing, according to Miller, they made the covenant a bargain or a contract binding upon both signatories. They furthermore made it the "foundation for the whole history and structure of Christian theology" in a way that would have made John Calvin turn in his grave.[10] This covenant theology sought to confine the unconfineable God in human terms and to give significance to man's moral and spiritual activity. Carried too far this could lead to a rationalism, on the one hand, in which all the mysteries were explained and, on the other, to a works-righteousness. Perry Miller writes, especially in his earlier works, that covenant theology had led to both results, so much so as to create a real gulf between Calvin and the marrow of Puritan divinity.[11] Reappraisals of Perry Miller tend to moderate both his understanding of Calvin and some of his conclusions concerning Puritanism.[12] Miller's later statement that covenant theology was an idiom in the development of Reformed theology seems to be more correct.

Covenant theology was essentially an effort to make sense out of the relationship of God and man. On the one hand, Antinomianism which left everything up to divine grace and on the other hand, Arminianism which gave too much credit to man's decision, had to be avoided. The Puritans knew that salvation was wholly the work of God; and they also knew that historically and psychologically, it was altogether the work of man. Covenant theology and the theology of the decrees of God were one way of attempting to do justice to both aspects of salvation. The Confession would deal with the same problem, perhaps more successfully, under the headings of justification and sanctification, as will be indicated in the next chapter.

THE CHRISTIAN LIFE

Christian faith is embodied finally not in a creed but in a human life and preeminently in the Christian community. No one in the Christian tradition understood this better than the Calvinists. The renewal of the image of God in man was a basic thrust of Calvin's theology. The Puritans had a deep awareness of man's need for purity of heart, and they were keen observers of Christian experience. It is not surprising that Chapters X through XXXIII, comprising two-thirds of the Confession, deal with the Christian life. When this section of the Confession is supplemented by the commentary on the Ten Commandments in the Larger Catechism, it is clear that the writers of the Confession were not simply concerned with sound doctrine but also with the embodiment of doctrine in life. William Ames had written that "theology is the doctrine or teaching of living to God."[1] John Calvin before him had insisted that the end of theology is the edification of the Christian man.[2] Later Calvinists would write "that truth is in order to goodness; and the great touchstone of truth, its tendency to promote holiness . . ."[3] Theology for Calvinists of all nuances is a practical not a theoretical science, and the end of theology is not the vision of God but a life obedient to his will.

This characteristic of the Reformed tradition can also be understood as an emphasis upon the work of the Holy Spirit. This is not immediately clear from reading Chapters XX through XXXIII of the Confession, as there are few references to the Spirit; but much of these sections is an elaboration of the effectual call which is accomplished by the Word and Spirit. The validity of the sacraments depends ultimately neither upon the faith of the administrator nor upon the faith of the recipient nor upon the elements, but upon the Spirit. Prayer is made with the help of the Spirit, and it is the Spirit that makes the ordinances of the church effective. The work of the Spirit is concrete, ethical, and even rational, not necessarily ecstatic or enthusiastic.

The origin of the Christian life is the predestinate love of

God that is realized in the "effectual calling" of God's Spirit (The Confession X). The Christian life is analyzed in terms of the "benefits" that flow from effectual calling. Seen from another perspective, these benefits can be called "stages" of the Christian life.[4] The eighth chapter of Romans was indelibly imprinted on the Reformed consciousness, especially the words of verse thirty, "And those whom he predestined he also called; and those whom he called he also justified; and those whom he justified he also glorified."[5] To this list the writers of the Confession added adoption and sanctification which also had good Pauline warrant.

Effectual calling is a restatement of the doctrine of predestination in terms of its historical actualization. Those whom God has predestined, he is pleased to call in his appointed and accepted time. The origin of the Christian life is with God. It is by grace alone, and it is accomplished by his Word and Spirit. The human counterpart to effectual calling is conversion. Thus effectual calling is an appropriate introduction to the final twenty-three chapters of the Confession, for these chapters describe the way God's effectual call is realized in the Christian life and community.

Justification and sanctification are two dimensions of one Christian experience of salvation. Justification is forgiveness, and sanctification is the renewal of life. Justification means that our finest achievements fall short of the glory of God and must be forgiven. Sanctification means the achievement of sainthood is the primary vocation of man. Justification is total and complete in the act of forgiveness. Sanctification is a process that is never complete or perfect in history. Those whom God calls he forgives and renews. Forgiveness and sanctification can never be separated, and they must never be confused.

The Confession puts together these two dimensions of Christian experience as well as they have ever been put together in the history of theology.[6] A brief reading of the Confession and especially of the Larger Catechism will immediately indicate how clearly the words have been defined and the issues delineated (The Confession XI, XIII, XIV). Yet the Reformed theologians, if they erred, generally erred on the side of sanctification. This bias may be the total impact of the Confession, for in addition to the chapter on sanctification the Confession also includes chapters on repentance, good works, and the law of God. The chapter on good works is especially well written, because of the ever-present danger of Antinomianism. The Antinomians had responded to the doctrines of predestination and justification by interpreting the whole of Christian life as grace and forgiveness and by omitting sanctification. The writers of the Confession intended that the Christian life must be understood as *both* forgiveness *and* renewal.

Adoption was emphasized by the Puritan theologians to describe the new situation of the called or the elect. The elect were now to enjoy all the rights and privileges of the children of God. As such, adoption is a synonym for justification, but it expresses personal nuances and dimensions of the experience that justification does not. Adoption also presupposes the changed heart of sanctification, but again this is expressed in a more personal way. Adoption into the family of God is a warmer, more human way of stating the faith than the more technical and abstract language of justification and sanctification.

Glorification is the fourth benefit of effectual calling. Glorification is the actualization of what is potential and only partially realized in sanctification. William Ames outlined four stages of glorification in his summary of Christian faith: (1) the apprehension and sense of the love of God shining forth in Christ, in the communion of believers with him; (2) the undoubting hope and expectation of the enjoyment of all those good things which God has prepared for his own; (3) the possession of spiritual gifts of grace in overflowing abundance; (4) the experience of God's benevolence or goodwill.[7] The Confession embodies this material in the chapters "Of the Perseverance of the Saints," "Of the Assurance of Grace and Salvation," "Of the Communion of the Saints." The consummation of glorification is the theme of the final two chapters, "Of the State of Man after Death, and Of the Resurrection of the Dead," and "Of the Last Judgment." After death "the souls [selves] of the righteous, being then made perfect in holiness, are received into the highest heavens, where they behold the face of God, in light and glory, waiting for the full redemption of their bodies . . ." (The Confession XXXI, 1)

The contemporary reader may be repelled by the abstract language of this analysis of Christian experience, and he may be convinced that the writers of the Confession knew too much about what happened after death. Yet the fact remains that this is a sober, empirical analysis of Christian experience that is still useful when translated into the idiom of contemporary language and experience.

The development of Christian life from its roots in effectual calling, with its counterpart in the human experience of conversion through justification, adoption, and sanctification to glorification, that is, the making perfect of redemption, is supplemented by chapters dealing with particular aspects or nuances of the Christian life. "Of Repentance Unto Life," "Of Saving Faith," "Of Good Works," and "Of the Law of God" have to do with dimensions of the Christian life. The chapters on the church, sacraments, and worship deal with life in the family of God. The remaining chapters on oaths and vows, on marriage and divorce, on Christian liberty and conscience, and on the state have to do with the public life of the Christian.

These chapters contain some of the most dated writings, some of the most difficult theologically, and some of the finest writings of the Confession. The chapter on saving faith is surely one of the weakest in the Confession as it contains a fundamental ambiguity as to the object of faith. It wavers between faith as believing that whatsoever is revealed in the Bible is true, and faith in God as he makes himself known in Jesus Christ. In Chapter XXXII the writers surely know too much about the state of man after death. The chapter on the state is dated in the power it gives the state in matters of religion. Nevertheless, these chapters also contain some of the finest statements of the Confession. "God alone is Lord of the conscience, and hath left it free from the doctrines and commandments of men which are in any thing contrary to His Word; or beside it, if [sic] matters of faith or worship. So that, to believe such doctrines, or to obey such commands, out of conscience, is to betray true liberty of conscience:

and the requiring of an implicit faith, and an absolute and blind
obedience is to destroy liberty of conscience, and reason also."
(The Confession XX, 2) Even if the writers of the Confession did
not fully actualize this paragraph in life, it must still be one of the
finest statements of its kind in confessional literature. Other fresh
and powerful statements are "Marriage was ordained for the
mutual help of husband and wife; . . ." ". . . it is the duty of
Christians to marry in the Lord . . ." (The Confession XXIV, 2,
3) "All saints, that are united to Jesus Christ . . . being united to
one another in love, they have communion in each other's gifts
and graces . . ." (The Confession XXVI, 1) "God, the supreme
Lord and King of all the world, hath ordained civil magistrates,
to be, under Him . . ." (The Confession XXIII, 1)

The chapters in the Confession on the Christian life are
supplemented by the exposition of the Ten Commandments in
the Larger Catechism. The Catechism first of all defines the law
of God and its role in human life. It then specifies how the law
is to be interpreted and applied to the human situation. It finally
engages in a thorough analysis of the Ten Commandments. The
Larger Catechism thus provides a manual of ethics, personal and
social. In some cases the ethics of the Larger Catechism are very
relative to its own time, as in the delineation of duties to inferiors,
equals, and superiors. In some cases the analysis is quaint, as in
the specification of the use of a "physick" (laxative) as part of the
obedience required by the sixth commandment, or when it also
requires "a sober use of meat." All in all the Christian life is
spelled out with a thoroughness and perceptiveness that no one
would attempt today. But contemporary modesty as to the nature
of the Christian life is certainly not all gain and is not likely to
duplicate the honesty and integrity of a society nurtured on the
Catechism.

Two-thirds of the Confession is devoted to an analytical
description of the Christian life and of its practices and respon-
sibilities in the world. The method is analytic rather than deductive, concrete and empirical rather than theoretical. Its primary
purpose is the glory of God, not the realization of man's identity
or potential or even the service of man. This ultimate purpose

was realized in the proximate purpose of the embodiment of
Christian faith in the life of a particular man and in society. Any
distinction between the individual man and society was unnecessary if not impossible in the 1640's. The Christian man and the
Holy Commonwealth were part of one understanding of the purposes of God in world history. Today it is easier to criticize the
failures of the Puritans than it is to duplicate their vision or to
rival their measure of actual achievement.

THE CONFESSION AS NORMATIVE THEOLOGY

The avowed purpose of the theological work of the Assembly was fourfold: to establish the life of the church in a way most agreeable to the Word of God; to clear the doctrine of the Church of England from aspersions and calumnies; to bring the doctrine and life of the church into nearer agreement with Reformed churches abroad; and to unite Britain under one confession. In order for these purposes to be accomplished, it was necessary for the theology of the Confession and Catechisms to be in some sense normative. The question is, "In what sense did the Assembly regard the theology of the Confession as normative?"

The Assembly was an advisory commission for Parliament. It never specifically declared how the Confession was to be used. The reason for this silence is possibly to be found in the fairly common theological agreement concerning doctrine. The heresies such as Arminianism, Antinomianism, and Socinianism were easily recognized and vigorously condemned by members of the Assembly. The subscription controversies would come later in the eighteenth century when the theological consensus was breaking down.

There is no evidence that members of the Assembly had any intention of exacting the kind of detailed subscription that some adherents of the Confession wished to demand at a later time. There is some convincing evidence that they did not wish this kind of subscription. Anthony Tuckney, who had as much to do with the writing of the Confession and Catechisms as any other, states very explicitly that this was not his intention. In correspondence with the Cambridge Platonist, Whichcote, he wrote: "For matter of 'improving-upon' I am not guilty. In the Assembly I gave my vote with others, that the Confession of Faith, putt-out by Authorities, should not bee required to bee eyther sworne or subscribed-too. Wee having bin burnt in the hand in that kind before: but so as not to be publically preached or written against; which is indeed contrarie to that liberty of prophesying which some call for; but, you say, you plead not for; though your second advice in your sermon seemed, in mine and other men's eyes, to look fullie that way. . . ."[1]

Whichcote had confronted Tuckney with a very difficult point in his argument. Unless the interpreter of Scripture is infallible, then great care must be exercised in any imposition of the creed. Tuckney was unwilling to admit an infallible interpreter, but likewise he was unwilling to draw the inevitable conclusions from the denial of an infallible interpreter. Whichcote maintained much the same position that Milton did in the *Areopagitica*. The maintenance of truth, Whichcote said, is God's charge; the maintenance of charity is ours. Tuckney thought that he detected something of Descartes' methodological doubt in Whichcote. A full religious toleration was further than Tuckney was willing to go.

Tuckney's statement must be further qualified by the fact that he and sixteen London ministers who were members of the Westminster Assembly signed *A Testimony to the Truth of Jesus Christ and to our Solemn League and Covenant* on December 14, 1647, that vigorously repudiated the error of toleration, patronizing and promoting all other errors, heresies, and blasphemies whatsoever under the grossly abused notion of Liberty of Conscience. They went on to say that "a publike and generall toleration will prove an hideous and complexive evil, of the most dangerous and mischievous consequence."[2] While Tuckney may have objected to a detailed subscription, it is a mistake to see in him or in most of the members of the Assembly any advocate of religious liberty. He did favor, as not only his statement to Whichcote but his respect for Whichcote confirms, a certain measure of theological freedom.

In a sermon entitled "On a Good Form of Sound Words," (1650) Tuckney defended confessions, catechisms, "summes," institutions, and "systems" by which theologians "lay down together such divine truths as are scattered up and down in the Scripture or explain such as there seem to be something obscure and so present them, in a full and clear distinct view, for the better help, especially of a weaker eye against the fascinations of jugling imposters."[3] Tuckney was also willing to have doctrine tested by its fruits. ". . . although the Scripture be the Rule, or Pole-Starre, yet the spirits of the faithful savingly touched from heaven point to it; so that it is likely to be an unsavory or poisonous weed, which the flock of Christ's sheep generally will let stand, and not feed on; and I should much suspect that either doctrine or practice, which the hearts of godly universally have an inward antipathy against: as on the contrary, 'It seemed good to the Holy Ghost and us,' was the ground and tenor of a synodical discussion in the best of times."[4] "It is likely," Tuckney concludes, "to be wholesome food which healthful sound men do generally and in a manner naturally relish and feed upon."[5] In this sermon Tuckney likewise testifies that he has known what it is to be pinched by imposition of doctrine and that he has no desire to impose upon others, though the freedom he is willing to grant falls short of the "liberty of prophesying advocated by some."

Something of the attitude of the Assembly may be reflected in Philip Nye's report that the Assembly voted down a proposal that the Catechism be subscribed.[6] In 1660 he also wrote concerning the Catechism, "The Shorter Catechism agreed upon by the Assembly of divines at Westminster and presented to the Honorable Houses of Parliament then sitting, and by them ordered to be printed and published, but no man enjoyned to use it or punishable if he made use of any other to instruct his people in. This little Book for the comprehensiveness of it, as also for exactness or order and expression, hath (as it deserves) a great esteeme with many learned men, notwithstanding to be the one and only Book, for all capacities that are to be instructed in principles, throughout the nations, is a perfection not to be expected from any common gift."[7]

Richard Baxter, one of the most influential Puritans of the seventeenth century but not a member of the Assembly, had a very lofty opinion of the Confession and Catechisms. "I truly profess, I take the labours of the Assembly, especially these three pieces . . . for the best Book, next my Bible, in my study."[8] Yet he did not hesitate to express his reservations about some formulations of the Assembly.[9] Stating that he did not know whether the Confession was intended as a test of doctrine, he went on to declare his opposition to any such use of a large and comprehensive confession. The Decalogue, the Apostles' Creed and the Lord's Prayer, he thought, were enough. Furthermore, the heart of the matter is the content of the doctrine, not the words or the formulas. Baxter summarizes his attitude toward the Confession in this way. "There is a singular use for a full body of theology, or a profession concluded on by such Reverend Assemblies, that the younger ministers may be taught by it, and the reverence of it may restrain them from rashly contradicting it: and there is a necessity of exercising power in Ministerial Assemblies, for the actual restraint of such as shall teach things intolerably unsound, and all ministers should there be accountable for their doctrine."[10]

The sustenance of theological integrity and theological freedom concomitantly is always difficult. Jeremy Taylor, whose *Liberty of Prophesying* (1647) was a strong statement of the case for freedom, later found that freedom was not easy.[11] Members of the Assembly were so sensitive to the problems of "Abominable errors, damnable heresies and horrid blasphemies" that they could speak of that "monster toleration."[12] Yet out of this tension came the conclusion that no man is good enough or wise enough to tell another man what his religion should be and that the Christian community is safest if different expressions of it are permitted to exist in the same society.[13] This still left the problem of the integrity of the community of faith itself.

The breakdown of the theological consensus of the seventeenth century was the occasion for bitter controversies in Britain, Ireland, and America about subscription to the Confession. Various formulas were used. The Adopting Act of American Presbyterians in 1729 specified that ministers declared their allegiance to the Confession *"as being in all essential and necessary articles, good forms of sound words and systems of Christian doctrine."*[14] In 1788 with the founding of the General Assembly, the adherence to the Confession was affirmed "as containing the system of doctrine taught in the holy scriptures."[15] The wisest interpretating of "system" is that of A. A. Hodge of Princeton. When one adopts the Confession as a system, according to Hodge, he is declaring that he accepts that in the Confession which constitutes him as Christian, Protestant, and Reformed in theology.[16]

The writers of the Confession took their faith seriously, and therefore they took heresy seriously. For them toleration was not a simple solution. It is a simple solution for many today, not because of a profounder faith, but because of a less serious regard for theology. Authentic toleration is always deeply embedded in life itself and combines passion for truth with the humility that confesses one's own truth is never *the* truth. In no age is this a simple achievement.

EPILOGUE—THEOLOGY AS DIALOGUE

The final assessment of the Westminster Confession is determined by the evaluator's understanding of the nature of the theological enterprise. The conclusion offered here is that theology can best be understood as dialogue and that the Westminster Confession is a very significant episode in the continuing theological dialogue of the church. As such, the Confession is entitled to be taken with utmost seriousness but not with idolatry. God alone is the Lord, and man's apprehension of his presence is never final. Richard Niebuhr has said it very well indeed.

> Beyond the dark powers, the Chthonian deities of the physical life of man, there are our Olympian gods—our country, our ideologies, our democracies, civilization, churches, our art which we practice for art's sake, our truth which we pursue for truth's sake, our moral values, our ideas and the social forces which we personalize, adore, and on which we depend for deliverance from sheer nothingness and the utter inconsequence of existence. . . .
>
> The causes for which we live all die. The great social movements pass and are supplanted by others. The ideals we fashion are revealed by time to be relative. The empire and the cities to which we are devoted all decay. At the end nothing is left to defend us against the void of meaninglessness.[1]

So it is with our creeds. They are human testimonies to the ineffable Reality that is the source and end of our existence.

Theology is by definition rational speech about God. It is logos (reason), not an enthusiastic utterance and certainly not an irrational utterance. It is not even what John Hutchison has called first-order religious language, that is, an immediate expression of religious experience as in prayer.[2] Anselm, the great theologian of the eleventh century, did write theology in the form of prayer,[3] but certainly this is possible only in the age of faith and in the community of faith. For the most part, theology must be second-order language, that is, reflective, critical, analytic language that describes, defines, and articulates the Christian faith in a precise and coherent fashion.

Theology in its broadest definition, as when God is defined in some attenuated fashion as man's ultimate concern, is critical reflection upon the meaning of human existence. In this sense every man is a theologian, though he may not be a critical or reflective theologian. Life is so constituted that it forces man to make decisions and to take actions every day that are finally based upon some faith commitment about the meaning of life and the universe. In a more carefully defined sense, theology may be Islamic theology, Shinto theology, or Christian theology, depending on its point of reference. For Christian theology, God is defined by Jesus Christ. This is a simple but adequate definition. For Christians, Jesus of Nazareth is the embodiment of the wisdom and the power of God. He is the intelligible event in the light of which all other events become intelligible. The task of Christian theology is to interpret human existence and to understand the meaning of the universe in the light of the revelation of God that comes to a focus in Jesus Christ. Christian theology is primarily dialogue with this revelation.

Christian theology, however, is not exclusively dialogue with the act of God in Jesus Christ, for man is no abstract, isolated entity. He is flesh and blood, living in a particular time and place. Hence there are further dimensions to the dialogue. There is dialogue with Christian tradition, that is, with the way other Christians in other times and places have understood this revelation. There is also dialogue with the experience of the Christian community. How has the revelation of God been experienced and appropriated in human life and in the experience of the community? There is dialogue with culture, with the sciences—physical, biological, and social. New discoveries in science enable the theologian to see new dimensions of the Christian revelation and to ask new questions. Social movements such as the emancipation of women have compelled theologians to hear and to see dimensions of the Christian revelation of which they were previously unaware. It may be that we are now entering a period when the religions of mankind will raise acute questions for the Christian theologian.[4] The dialogical circle of the theologian is very large, even though the revelation in Jesus Christ is the decisive and central focus of the dialogue.

The theological dialogue is simply the attempt to articulate in clear, precise, and coherent terms the meaning and purpose of human existence for those who believe that ultimate Reality has been finally disclosed in Jesus of Nazareth. The dialogue never ends because man's apprehension of the truth of God is always partial, limited, fragmentary. The context in which the dialogue takes place is always changing. New questions are being raised, and new movements and issues cry out for interpretation. Theology is written for time, not for eternity, and must be done over and over again.

The Westminster Confession can best be understood as an episode in the continuing dialogue of Christian theology. It is a particularly notable achievement of the dialogue. It states the faith with a perceptiveness of issues, a deftness of nuance, a clarity and precision of definition, a chasteness and economy of words that has seldom been equaled, much less surpassed. It combines in one coherent statement pure doctrine and ethics, theory and practice. In one sense it does the job too well, for its adherents begin to think of it as the final statement of the faith. Perhaps this is one reason the Reformed tradition produced so few theologians of stature in the eighteenth century.

Those who stand in the Reformed tradition, especially the English-speaking tradition, have been shaped by the Westminster Confession as by no other Christian creed. Even in rebellion against it, men have been formed by it. The Confession has its place alongside the other great Reformed creeds, such as the Second Helvetic Confession, the Scots Confession of 1560, and the French Confession of 1559. Only those who have learned to appreciate its excellence as a statement of the Reformed faith can either understand the faith or merit the right to criticize the Confession negatively. No modern confession is likely to rival it in technical excellence.

NOTES

INTRODUCTION

1. The Assembly receives slight or no notice at all in Maurice Ashley, *England in the Seventeenth Century (1603–1714)*, third edition (Baltimore: Penguin Books Inc., 1963); Meyrick H. Carré, *Phases of Thought in England* (Oxford: The Clarendon Press, 1949); *The English Revolution, 1600–1660*, ed. E. W. Ives (New York: Harper Torchbook, 1968).
2. Williston Walker, *The Creeds and Platforms of Congregationalism* (New York: Charles Scribner's Sons, 1893), pp. 354, 185, 439, 501.
3. William L. Lumpkin, *Baptist Confessions of Faith* (Valley Forge, Pennsylvania: Judson Press, 1959).
4. Reinhold Niebuhr, *The Irony of American History* (New York: Charles Scribner's Sons, 1952), pp. vii–viii.

THE HISTORICAL CHARACTER OF CREEDS

1. Karl Barth, *Theology and Church, Shorter Writings 1920–1928* (New York: Harper & Row, Publishers, 1962), p. 112.
2. Philip Schaff, *The Creeds of Christendom*, 3 vols. (New York: Harper Brothers, 1919), vol. 1, pp. 389–390.
3. *Creeds of the Churches*, ed. John H. Leith (Garden City: Doubleday & Co., 1963), pp. 127 ff.; Schaff, *The Creeds of Christendom*, vol. 1, pp. 354–813.
4. Schaff, *The Creeds of Christendom*, vol. 1, pp. 220–353.
5. Paul Jacobs, *Theologie Reformierter Bekenntnisschriften im Grundzügen* (Neukirchener Verlag, 1959), pp. 9 ff.
6. *The Harmony of Protestant Confessions*, ed. Peter Hall (London: John F. Shaw, 1842). For the role of Beza, see Paul F. Geisendorf, *Théodore de Bèze* (Geneva: Labor & Fides, 1949), pp. 337 ff.
7. See especially the Introduction to *Minutes of the Sessions of the Westminster Assembly of Divines*, eds. Alex F. Mitchell and John Struthers (Edinburgh: William Blackwood & Sons, 1874) and Alex F. Mitchell, "The Theology of the Reformed Churches with Special Reference to the Westminster Standards" in *Report of Proceedings of the Second General Council of Presbyterian Alliance, Convened at Philadelphia, September, 1880*, eds. John B. Dales and R. M. Patterson (Philadelphia: Presbyterian Journal Company, 1880), pp. 474–484.

THE POLITICAL CONTEXT

1. For a brief summary of the interpretations of the period see: Philip A. M. Taylor, *The Origins of the English Civil War: Conspiracy, Crusade, or Class Conflict* (Boston: D. C. Heath & Co., 1960). Our age can only with difficulty understand the importance of preaching and literature in the century preceding Westminster. Great preachers were given the public adulation that is reserved today for entertainers. Forty-three percent of the books that came from English presses from the time of Claxton to 1641 had a religious theme. See Louis B. Wright, "The Significance of Religious Writings in the English Renaissance," *Journal of History of Ideas* I, no. 1 (January 1940): 59–68.

2. William Haller, *The Rise of Puritanism* (New York: Harper Torchbooks, 1957).
3. *Ibid.* pp. 324 ff. Cf. Alex F. Mitchell, *The Westminster Assembly, Its History and Standards* (Philadelphia: Presbyterian Board of Publication, 1884), p. 97.
4. *The Constitutional Documents of the Puritan Revolution 1625–1660*, ed. Samuel Rawson Gardiner, third edition (Oxford: The Clarendon Press, 1906), p. 229.
5. Mitchell, *The Westminster Assembly*, pp. ix–xii.
6. See S. W. Carruthers, *Everyday Work of the Westminster Assembly* (Philadelphia: Presbyterian Historical Society, 1943), pp. 105 ff.
7. Anthony Tuckney, *Forty Sermons upon Several Occasions* (London, 1676), p. 237.
8. Mitchell, *The Westminster Assembly*, pp. 156 ff; John Lightfoot, *The Whole Works of the Rev. John Lightfoot, D. D.*, ed. John Rogers Pitman, 13 vols. (London: Hatchard & Son, 1824), vol. 13, p. 17.
9. *The Constitutional Documents of the Puritan Revolution 1624–1660*, Gardiner, p. 268.
10. Lightfoot, *The Whole Works of the Rev. John Lightfoot*, vol. 13, p. 15.
11. The Erastians generally favor greater power of the state in affairs of the church and limited church power to moral suasion. For a general discussion of Erastianism see W. K. Jordan, *The Development of Religious Toleration in England*, 4 vols. (Cambridge: Harvard Univ. Press, 1940), vol. 4, pp. 265 ff.
12. Mitchell, *The Westminster Assembly*, p. 12.
13. Robert Baillie, *The Letters and Journals of Robert Baillie 1637–1662*, ed. David Laing, 3 vols. (Edinburgh: Robert Ogle, 1841), vol. 2, p. 186. The author's spellings.

THE CULTURAL CONTEXT

1. Arthur Lovejoy, *The Great Chain of Being; A Study of the History of an Idea* (Cambridge: Harvard Univ. Press, 1936).
2. Edward, Lord Herbert of Cherbury, *De Veritate*, trans. with an intro. by Meyrick H. Carré (Bristol: Univ. of Bristol, 1937).
3. Anthony Tuckney, *Forty Sermons upon Several Occasions* (London, 1676).
4. Basil Willey, *The Seventeenth Century Background* (Garden City: Doubleday & Co., 1953), p. 139.
5. Herbert Butterfield, *The Origins of Modern Science 1300–1800* (London: G. Bell & Sons Ltd., 1950), pp. 77 ff; Alfred North Whitehead, *Science and the Modern World* (Cambridge: The Univ. Press, 1932), pp. 9–10.
6. Willey, *The Seventeenth Century Background*, pp. 11 ff.
7. *Minutes of the Sessions of the Westminster Assembly*, Mitchell and Struthers.
8. Anthony Tuckney, *None But Christ or a Sermon upon Acts 4:12*, Preached at St. Maries in Cambridge, on Commencement Sabbath, July 4, 1652 (London: John Rothwell and S. Gllibrand, 1654).
9. Edward, Lord Herbert of Cherbury, *De Veritate*.
10. W. K. Jordan, *The Development of Religious Toleration in England*, 4 vols. (Cambridge: Harvard Univ. Press, 1940), vol. 4, pp. 478 ff.
11. A. R. Hall, *The Scientific Revolution 1500–1800: The Formation of the Modern Scientific Attitude* (Boston: The Beacon Press, 1954, pp. 159 ff.
12. Whitehead, *Science and the Modern World*, pp. 49 ff.
13. *Ibid.*, p. 58.

14. T. Sprat, *The History of the Royal Society of London, 1667*, eds. J.I. Cope and H.W. Jones (St. Louis: Washington Univ. Press, 1958), p. 55, Appendix p. 65. Henry Lyons, *The Royal Society 1660–1940, A History of its Administration under its Charters* (Cambridge: The University Press, 1944), pp. 8–11.

15. Douglas Bush, *English Literature in the Earlier Seventeenth Century 1600–1660* (Oxford: The Clarendon Press, 1945), p. 270.

16. John Dillenberger, *Protestant Thought and Natural Science* (Garden City: Doubleday & Co., 1960), pp. 104 ff.

THE THEOLOGICAL CONTEXT

1. Alex F. Mitchell, *The Westminster Assembly, Its History and Standards* (Philadelphia: Presbyterian Board of Publication, 1884), p. ix.
    When the Assembly presented the Confession to Parliament, it wanted action to indicate to Protestant churches abroad as well as within the kingdom that Parliament never intended to innovate in matters of faith. *Minutes of the Sessions of the Westminster Assembly of Divines*, eds. Alex F. Mitchell and John Struthers (Edinburgh: William Blackwood & Sons, 1874), p. 291.

2. Paul S. Seaver, *The Puritan Lectureships; The Politics of Religious Dissent 1560–1662* (Stanford: Stanford Univ. Press, 1970).

3. Mitchell, *The Westminster Assembly*.

4. S. W. Carruthers, *Everyday Work of the Westminster Assembly* (Philadelphia: Presbyterian Historical Society, 1943), p. 106.

5. *Minutes of the Sessions of the Westminster Assembly*, Mitchell and Struthers, pp. 150 ff.

6. *Ibid.*, p. 151.

7. Meyrick H. Carré, *Phases of Thought in England* (Oxford: The Clarendon Press, 1949), p. 224.

8. Mitchell, *The Westminster Assembly*, pp. 326 ff.

9. *Dictionary of National Biography*, ed. Sidney Lee and others, 63 vols. (New York: The Macmillan Co., 1899), vol. 57, p. 397.

10. Anthony Tuckney, *Forty Sermons upon Several Occasions* (London, 1676); John Arrowsmith, *Armilla Catechetica: A Chain of Principles* (Cambridge: John Field, 1659).

11. Carré, *Phases of Thought in England*, p. 189.

12. Charles Davis Cremeans, *The Reception of Calvinist Thought in England* (Urbana: Univ. of Illinois Press, 1949).

13. See Henry Bullinger, *The Decades of Henry Bullinger*, ed. Thomas Harding, 4 vols. (Cambridge: The Univ. Press, 1850).

14. Cremeans, *The Reception of Calvinist Thought*, p. 82.

15. *Ibid.*, p. 65.

16. *Ibid.*, p. 82.

17. Hales' letters make vivid the acrimonies and arrogance of the orthodox at Dort. In the preface to the *Golden Remains* his friend Anthony Farindon wrote: "You may please to take notice that in his younger days he was a Calvinist and even then when he was employed at that Synod, and at the well pressing 3 S. John 16 by Episcopius—There, I bid John Calvin good night, as he often told me."

18. "Unhappilie Amiraut's Questions are brought in on our Assemblie. Many more loves these fancies here than I did expect. It falls out ill that Spanhim's

book is so long a-coming out, whileas Amiraut's treatise goes in the Assemblie from hand to hand; yet I hope this shall goe right." Robert Baillie, *The Letters and Journals of Robert Baillie 1637–1662*, ed. David Laing, 3 vols. (Edinburgh: Robert Ogle, 1841), vol. 2, p. 324.

19. John Calvin, *Institutes of the Christian Religion*, ed. John T. McNeill, trans. Ford Lewis Battles, 2 vols. (Philadelphia: The Westminster Press, 1960), vol. 1, I, 1.

20. Baillie, *The Letters and Journals*, vol. 2, pp. 81 ff.

21. *Minutes of the Sessions of the Westminster Assembly*, Mitchell and Struthers.

22. Baillie, *The Letters and Journals*, vol. 3, Appendix p. 451.

23. H. John McLachlan, *Socinianism in Seventeenth-Century England* (Oxford: Oxford Univ. Press, 1951), pp. 9 ff.

THE MEMBERS OF THE ASSEMBLY AND THEIR WORK

1. Charles A. Briggs, "A Documentary History of the Westminster Assembly," *The Presbyterian Review* I, (January 1880): 134 ff.

2. Robert Baillie, *The Letters and Journals of Robert Baillie 1637–1662*, ed. David Laing, 3 vols. (Edinburgh: Robert Ogle, 1841), vol. 2, p. 111.

3. Baillie, *The Letters and Journals*, vol. 2, p. 110.

4. William Orme, *A Life of Richard Baxter and a Critical Examination of His Writings* in "The Practical Works of the Rev. Richard Baxter," 23 vols. (London, 1830), vol. 1, p. 69.

5. *Ibid.*, pp. 70–71. Orme includes negative comments from Lord Clarendon's *History of the Rebellion* and from John Milton's "Fragment of a History of England."

6. *Dictionary of National Biography*, ed. Sidney Lee and others, 63 vols. (New York: The Macmillan Co., 1953), vol. 58, pp. 286–287.

7. *Ibid.*

8. *Minutes of the Sessions of the Westminster Assembly of Divines*, eds. Alex F. Mitchell and John Struthers (Edinburgh: William Blackwood & Sons, 1874), p. 168.

9. Samuel William Carruthers, *Three Centuries of the Westminster Shorter Catechism* (Fredericton, N.B.: Univ. of New Brunswick, 1957), p. 5.

10. *Dictionary of National Biography*, Sidney Lee and others, vol. 58, p. 286.

11. Anthony Tuckney, *Forty Sermons upon Several Occasions* (London, 1676).

12. *Ibid.*, p. 170.

13. *Ibid.*, p. 188.

14. *Ibid.*

15. *Ibid.*

16. John Arrowsmith, *Armilla Catechetica: A Chain of Principles* (Cambridge: John Field, 1659).

17. See J. Minton Batten, *John Dury, Advocate of Christian Reunion* (Chicago: The Univ. of Chicago Press, 1944).

18. John Dury, *A model of church-government* (By T. R. and E. M. for John Bellamy, 1647), pp. 8–9.

19. *Minutes of the Westminster Assembly*, Mitchell and Struthers, p. 507; cf. Jacob Acontius, *Satans Stratagems* (London: John Macock, 1648). See the Appendix for Dury's comments.

20. *Dictionary of National Biography*, Sidney Lee and others, vol. 59, pp. 141–145.

21. John Wallis, *A brief and easie explanation of the shorter catechism,* eighth edition (London: Peter Parker, 1662).

22. Alex Mitchell, *The Westminster Assembly, Its History and Standards* (Philadelphia: Presbyterian Board of Publication, 1884), p. 183.

23. *Ibid.,* pp. 121–122.

24. *Ibid.,* p. 429.

25. Baillie, *The Letters and Journals,* vol. 2, pp. 184–185. Author's spellings.

26. *Minutes of the Sessions of the Westminster Assembly,* Mitchell and Struthers, p. 105.

27. Baillie, *The Letters and Journals; Minutes of the Sessions of the Westminster Assembly,* Mitchell and Struthers, p. 110; John Lightfoot, *The Whole Works of the Rev. John Lightfoot,* ed. John Rogers Pitman (London: J. F. Dove, 1824), vol. 13, pp. 10, 256, 267.

28. Baillie, *The Letters and Journals,* vol. 2, pp. 107–109.

29. Lightfoot, *The Whole Works of the Rev. John Lightfoot,* vol. 13, pp. 299–301.

THE WRITING OF THE CONFESSION

1. John Lightfoot, *The Whole Works of the Rev. John Lightfoot,* ed. John Rogers Pitman, 13 vols. (London: J. F. Dove, 1824), vol. 13, p. 5.

2. Robert Baillie, *The Letters and Journals of Robert Baillie 1637–1662,* ed. David Laing, 3 vols. (Edinburgh: Robert Ogle, 1841), vol. 2, p. 90.

3. *The Constitutional Documents of the Puritan Revolution 1625–1660,* ed. Samuel Rawson Gardiner (Oxford: The Clarendon Press, 1958), p. 267; Robert Low Orr, *Alexander Henderson, Churchman and Statesman* (London: Hodder and Stoughton, 1919), pp. 298 ff.

4. *The Constitutional Documents,* Gardiner, pp. 268–269.

5. *Minutes of the Sessions of the Westminster Assembly of Divines,* eds. Alex F. Mitchell and John Struthers (Edinburgh: William Blackwood & Sons, 1874) p. ixxxvii.

6. *Ibid.,* pp. 75 ff.

7. *Ibid.,* p. 77.

8. B. B. Warfield, *The Westminster Assembly and Its Work* (New York: Oxford Univ. Press, 1931), p. 86.

9. Jack Bartlett Rogers, *Scripture in the Westminster Confession* (Grand Rapids: William B. Eerdmans Pub. Co., 1967), pp. 158–159; *Minutes of the Sessions of the Westminster Assembly,* Mitchell and Struthers, p. 83.

10. *Minutes of the Sessions of the Westminster Assembly,* Mitchell and Struthers, p. 91.

11. *Ibid.,* pp. 110–115.

12. *Ibid.,* p. 115.

13. *Ibid.,* p. 114.

14. *Ibid.,* p. 164.

15. *Ibid.,* p. 190.

16. *Ibid.*

17. *Ibid.,* pp. 110, 168, 245.

18. Warfield, *The Westminster Assembly and Its Work,* p. 96; Lightfoot, *The Whole Works of the Rev. John Lightfoot,* vol. 13, pp. 3–4:

    The Confession was written under the rules that Parliament had established for the Assembly in 1643; they were designed to maintain responsible debate.

(1) That two Assessors be joined to the Prolocutor, to supply his place in case of absence or infirmity.

(2) That Scribes be appointed, to set down all proceedings, and those to be Divines, who are not of the Assembly, viz. Mr. *Henry Robens* and Mr. *Adonitan Byfield.*

(3) Every member, at his first entry into the Assembly, shall make serious and solemn protestation, not to maintain any thing but what he believes to be truth in sincerity, when discovered unto him.

(4) No resolution to be given upon any question the same day, wherein it is first propounded.

(5) What any man undertakes to prove as necessary, he shall make good out of Scripture.

(6) No man to proceed in any dispute, after the Prolocutor has enjoined him silence, unless the Assembly desire he may go on.

(7) No man to be denied to enter his dissent from the Assembly, and his reasons for it, in any point, after it hath been first debated in the Assembly, and thence (if the dissenting party desire it) to be sent to the Houses of Parliament by the Assembly, not by any particular man or men, in a private way, when either House shall require.

(8) All things agreed on and prepared for the Parliament, to be openly read and allowed in the Assembly, and then offered as the judgment of the Assembly, if the major part assent. Provided that the opinion of any persons dissenting, and the reasons urged for it, be annexed thereunto, if the dissenters require it, together with the solutions, if any were given to the Assembly, to these reasons.

The protestation that was taken on July 8, 1643 in fulfillment of the third rule declared:

"I, A.B. do seriously and solemnly protest, in the presence of Almighty God, that in this Assembly, whereof I am a member, I will not maintain any thing in matters of doctrine, but what I think in my conscience to be truth; or in point of discipline, but what I shall conceive to conduce most to the glory of God, and the good and peace of his church."

Cf. *Journals of the House of Commons,* July 5, 1643, vol. 3, p. 157.

19. *Minutes of the Sessions of the Westminster Assembly,* Mitchell and Struthers, p. 290.
20. *Ibid.,* p. 303.
21. *Minutes of the Sessions of the Westminster Assembly,* Mitchell and Struthers, p. 349.
22. Alex F. Mitchell, *The Westminster Assembly, Its History and Standards* (Philadelphia: Presbyterian Board of Publication, 1884), pp. 367–368; Baillie, *Letters and Journals,* vol. 2, p. 415; *Minutes of the Sessions of the Westminster Assembly,* Mitchell and Struthers, pp. 319–322, 336, 345.
23. *Minutes of the Sessions of the Westminster Assembly,* Mitchell and Struthers, p. 416.
24. *Ibid.,* 416–417.
25. William A. Shaw, *A History of the English Church, During the Civil War and Under the Commonwealth 1640–1660,* 2 vols. (New York: Franklin, Burt, Pub., 1970), vol. 2, p. 86.
26. *Ibid.,* p. 417.
27. *Minutes of the Sessions of the Westminster Assembly,* Mitchell and Struthers, p. 420.
28. *Ibid.,* p. 421.
29. William Haller, *Liberty and Reformation in the Puritan Revolution* (New York:

Columbia Univ. Press, 1955), pp. 103–104; cf. Ethyn Williams Kirby, "The English Presbyterians in the Westminster Assembly," *Church History* 33, no. 4 (December 1964): 418–428.

30. W. K. Jordan, *The Development of Religious Toleration in England*, 4 vols. (Cambridge: Harvard Univ., 1940), vol. 4, pp. 478 ff.

THE THEOLOGICAL METHOD: MODIFIED SCHOLASTICISM

1. Ten Theses of Berne, 1528; First Helvetic Confession, 1536; Lausanne Articles, 1536
2. French Confession, 1559; The Second Helvetic Confession, 1566; The Scots Confession of 1560
3. Brief summaries of various interpretations of the nature of Protestant scholasticism may be found in Robert P. Scharlemann, *Thomas Aquinas and John Gerhard* (New Haven: Yale Univ. Press, 1964).
4. See Cornelius Burges, *The fire of the sanctuarie newly uncovered or a compleat tract of zeale* (London, 1625), pp. 5–6.
5. See Otto W. Heick and J. L. Neve, *A History of Christian Thought*, 2 vols. (Philadelphia: Fortress Press, 1965), vol. 1, pp. 458 ff., pp. 474 ff.
6. *Creeds of the Churches*, ed. John H. Leith (Garden City: Doubleday & Co., 1963), p. 310.
7. See Paul Tillich, *Systematic Theology*, 3 vols. (Chicago: Univ. of Chicago Press, 1951), vol. 1, p. 54; cf. Karl Barth's foreword in Heinrich Heppe, *Reformed Dogmatics, Set out and Illustrated from the sources*, rev. and ed. Ernst Bizer, trans. G. T. Thomson (London: Allen & Unwin Ltd., 1950).
8. Scharlemann, *Thomas Aquinas and John Gerhard*, p. 14.
9. Brian G. Armstrong, *Calvinism and the Amyraut Heresy: Protestant Scholasticism and Humanism in Seventeenth-Century France* (Madison: Univ. of Wisconsin Press, 1969), p. 32.
10. William Ames, *The Marrow of Theology*, trans. from the third Latin edition, 1629, and ed. John D. Eusden (Boston: Pilgrim Press, 1968), p. 69.
11. William Temple, *A logical analysis of twentie select psalmes* (London: Thomas Man, 1605).
12. William Ames, *Conscience with the power and cases thereof* (London, 1639).
13. See pp. 83 ff. of the text.
14. *Minutes of the Sessions of the Westminster Assembly of Divines*, eds. Alex F. Mitchell and John Struthers (Edinburgh: William Blackwood & Sons, 1874), p. 158.
15. Selections from John Milton's *Areopagitica*.
16. Reinhold Niebuhr, *The Nature and Destiny of Man*, 2 vols. (New York: Charles Scribner's Sons, 1943), vol. 2, p. 217.
17. David Masson, *The Life of John Milton*, 6 vols. (London: Macmillan & Co., 1873), vol. 3, pp. 468–471. According to Masson, A. S. is Adam Stewart, an advocate of strict presbytery; Edwards is Edwards of the Gangroena; Scotch What d'ye call is Robert Baillie, though some think him George Gillespie.

THE BIBLE

1. The Scots Confession of 1560, The French Confession and the Belgic Confession, for example, begin with chapters on God.
2. John Lightfoot, *The Whole Works of the Rev. John Lightfoot*, ed. John Rogers Pitman, 13 vols. (London: J. F. Dove, 1824), vol. 13, p. 4.

 3. B. B. Warfield, *The Westminster Assembly and Its Work* (New York: Oxford Univ. Press, 1931), p. 155.
 4. Jack Bartlett Rogers, *Scripture in the Westminster Confession: A Problem of Historical Interpretation for American Presbyterianism* (Grand Rapids: William B. Eerdmans Co., 1967), p. 269.
 5. See Rogers, *Scripture in the Westminster Confession*, p. 301.
 6. See issues of *Presbyterian Review*. Cf. Charles A. Briggs, *Whither, A Theological Question for the Times* (New York: Charles Scribner's Sons, 1889); Lefferts A. Loetscher, *The Broadening Church, a Study of Theological Issues in the Presbyterian Church Since 1869* (Philadelphia: Univ. of Pennsylvania Press, 1954).
 7. *Minutes of the Sessions of the Westminster Assembly of Divines*, eds. Alex F. Mitchell and John Struthers (Edinburgh: William Blackwood & Sons, 1874), pp. 227–228.
 8. *A Directory For the Public Worship of God:* "Of the Preaching of the Word"; cf. John F. Wilson, *Pulpit in Parliament, Puritanism during the English Civil Wars 1640–1648* (Princeton, N. J.: Princeton Univ. Press, 1969).
 9. Second Helvetic Confession, chapter 2; Henry Bullinger, *The Decades of Henry Bullinger*, ed. Thomas Harding, 4 vols. (Cambridge: The Univ. Press, 1849), vol. 1, pp. 70 ff.
10. Bullinger, *The Decades*, vol. 1, pp. 70 ff.
11. *Minutes of the Sessions of the Westminster Assembly*, Mitchell and Struthers, pp. 227–228.
12. Augustine, *On Christian Doctrine*, trans. D. W. Robertson, Jr. (Indianapolis: The Bobbs-Merrill Company, Inc., 1958), p. 68.
13. George Gillespie, "Treatise of Miscellany Questions" in *The Presbyterian's Armory*, 3 vols. (Edinburgh: Robert Ogle & Oliver & Boyd, 1846), vol. 2, pp. 100–101.
14. Alfred North Whitehead, *Science and the Modern World* (Cambridge: The Univ. Press, 1932), p. 64.

THE LORDSHIP AND THE SOVEREIGNTY OF GOD

 1. Perry Miller and Thomas H. Johnson, *The Puritans* (Boston: American Book Company, 1938), p. 60.
 2. E. A. Burtt, *The Metaphysical Foundations of Modern Physical Science*, revised edition (Garden City: Doubleday & Co., 1949), pp. 61 ff.
 3. *Ibid.*, p. 236.
 4. Lord Eustace Percy, *John Knox* (Richmond: John Knox, n.d.), p. 109.
 5. *Ibid.*
 6. Christopher Dawson, *The Judgment of Nations* (New York: Sheed and Ward, 1942), pp. 44 ff.
 7. James C. Spalding, "Sermons Before Parliament (1640–1649) As a Public Puritan Diary," *Church History* 36, no. 1 (March 1967): 24–25.
 8. John F. Wilson, *Pulpit in Parliament; Puritanism during the English Civil Wars* (Princeton, N.J.: Princeton Univ. Press, 1969), p. 199.
 9. *Minutes of the Sessions of the Westminster Assembly of Divines*, eds. Alex F. Mitchell and John Struthers (Edinburgh: William Blackwood & Sons, 1874), p. 150.
10. Edward D. Morris, *Theology of the Westminster Symbols, A Commentary, Historical,*

Doctrinal, Practical on the Confession of Faith and Catechism and the related formularies of the Presbyterian Churches (Columbus, Ohio: 1900), p. 181.

11. E.g. John Calvin, *Institutes of the Christian Religion*, ed. John T. McNeill, trans. Ford Lewis Battles, 2 vols. (Philadelphia: The Westminster Press, 1960), vol. 2, VII, 5; vol. 1, XVII, 3.

THE COVENANT THEOLOGY

1. E.g. the doctrines of creation, sin, etc.
2. John Calvin, *Institutes of the Christian Religion*, ed. John T. McNeill, trans. Ford Lewis Battles, 2 vols. (Philadelphia: The Westminster Press, 1960), vol. 2, pp. 9–11.
3. E.g. Calvin's sermons on Deuteronomy and his commentary on Genesis 17.
4. Henry Bullinger, *The Decades of Henry Bullinger*, ed. Thomas Harding, 4 vols. (Cambridge: The Univ. Press, 1849), vol. 2, pp. 169–170.
5. Heinrich Heppe, *Reformed Dogmatics, Set out and Illustrated from the sources*, rev. and ed. Ernst Bizer, trans. G. T. Thomson (London: Allen & Unwin Ltd., 1950), pp. 281 ff.
6. See Robert Rollock, *Selected Works of Robert Rollock*, ed. William M. Gunn (Edinburgh: Woodrow Society, 1849), pp. 33 ff; for the development of covenant theology among Puritans see Jens G. Møller, "The Beginnings of Puritan Covenant Theology," *The Journal of Ecclesiastical History* 14, no. 1 (April 1963): 46–67; as well as Leonard J. Trinterud, "The Origins of Puritanism," *Church History* 20, no. 1 (March 1951): 37–57.
7. John Ball, *The Covenant of Grace* (London, 1645).
8. B. B. Warfield, *The Westminster Assembly and Its Work* (New York: Oxford Univ. Press, 1931), p. 56.
9. Perry Miller, *Errand into the Wilderness* (Cambridge: Harvard Univ. Press, 1956), p. 49.
10. *Ibid.*, p. 60.
11. *Ibid.*, pp. 48 ff.
12. George M. Marsden, "Perry Miller's Rehabilitation of the Puritans: A Critique," *Church History* 39, no. 1 (March 1970): 91–105; Everett H. Emerson, "Calvin and Covenant Theology," *Church History* 25, no. 2 (June 1956): 136–143.

THE CHRISTIAN LIFE

1. William Ames, *The Marrow of Theology*, trans. from the third Latin edition, 1629, and ed. John D. Eusden (Boston: Pilgrim Press, 1968), p. 77.
2. See unpublished Yale University dissertation "A Study of John Calvin's Doctrine of the Christian Life," by John H. Leith, pp. 6–8.
3. The Constitution of the United Presbyterian Church in the United States of America, Part II, Book of Order (Philadelphia: The Office of the General Assembly, 1967), 31.04.
4. See Introduction by John D. Eusden to William Ames, *The Marrow of Theology*, pp. 29 ff.
5. Romans 8:30. RSV

6. Reinhold Niebuhr, *The Nature and Destiny of Man*, 2 vols. (New York: Charles Scribner's Sons, 1943), vol. 2, p. 200.

7. Ames, *The Marrow of Theology*, pp. 172–174.

THE CONFESSION AS NORMATIVE THEOLOGY

1. Benjamin Whichcote, *Moral and Religious Aphorisms, To which are added eight letters which passed between Dr. Whichcote and Dr. Tuckney*, ed. Samuel Salter (London, 1753).

2. *A Testimony to the Truth of Jesus Christ and To Our Solemn League and Covenant; as also Against the Errors, Heresies and Blasphemies of these times, and the Toleration of them*. Subscribed by the Ministers of Christ within the Province of London, December 14, 1647 (London: Tho. Underhill, 1648).

3. Anthony Tuckney, *A Good Day Well Improved or Five Sermons upon Acts 9:31*. Two of which were Preached at Pauls, and Ordered to be Printed. To which is annexed a Sermon on 2 Tim. 1:13, Preached at St. Maries in Cambridge, on Commencement Sabbath, June 30, 1650 (London: J.F. for S. Gellibrand, 1656), pp. 247–248.

4. *Ibid.*, pp. 274–275.

5. *Ibid.*, p. 275.

6. *Conscientious Non Conformity* (1737), p. 77.

7. Philip Nye, *Beames of Former Light, Discovering How Evil it is to Impose Doubtful and Disputable Formes and Practices upon Ministers, Especially Under Penalty of Ejection for Non Conformity unto the same, as also something about catechising* (London: Adoniram Byfield, 1660).

8. Richard Baxter, *Richard Baxter's Confession of His Faith, Especially Concerning the Interest of Repentance and Sincere Obedience to Christ, in our Justification and Salvation* (London: Tho. Underhill and Fra Tyton, 1655), p. 22.

9. *Ibid.*

10. *Ibid.*, p. 27.

11. John Tulloch, *Rational Theology and Christian Philosophy in England in the Seventeenth Century*, 2 vols. (Hildesheim: Georg Olms Verlagsbuchhandlung, 1966), vol. 1, pp. 344 ff.

12. *A Testimony to the Truth of Jesus Christ and to Our Solemn League and Covenant.*

13. Winthrop S. Hudson, "Denominationalism as a Basis for Ecumenicity: A Seventeenth Century Conception," *Church History* 24, no. 1 (March 1955): 32–50.

14. Charles A. Briggs, *American Presbyterianism* (New York: Charles Scribner's Sons, 1885), p. 218; Leonard J. Trinterud, *The Forming of An American Tradition, A Reexamination of Colonial Presbyterianism* (Philadelphia: The Westminster Press, 1949), pp. 38 ff.

15. Trinterud, *Ibid.* p. 301.

16. A. A. Hodge, *A Commentary on the Confession of Faith* (Philadelphia: Presbyterian Board of Education, 1869), p. 542.

EPILOGUE—THEOLOGY AS DIALOGUE

1. H. Richard Niebuhr, *Radical Monotheism and Western Culture, With Supplementary Essays* (New York: Harper and Brothers, 1960), pp. 120, 122.

2. John A. Hutchison, *Language and Faith: Studies in Sign, Symbol, and Meaning* (Philadelphia: The Westminster Press, 1963), pp. 227 ff.

3. *A Scholastic Miscellany: Anselm to Ockham*, ed. and trans. Eugene R. Fairweather, The Library of Christian Classics, 26 vols. (Philadelphia: The Westminster Press, 1956), vol. 10, pp. 70 ff.

4. Wilfred Cantwell Smith, *The Faith of Other Men* (New York: Harper & Row, 1972), pp. 115 ff; Paul Tillich, *The Future of Religions* (New York: Harper & Row, 1966).

A Selected Bibliography

DOCUMENTS AND MINUTES OF THE WESTMINSTER ASSEMBLY

1. Carruthers, S. W. *The Westminster Confession of Faith, Being an account of the Preparation and Printing of its Seven Leading Editions To which is appended a Critical Text of the Confession with notes thereon.* Manchester: R. Aikman and Son, 1937.
   Provides critical text of the Confession.

2. Mitchell, Alex F. and Struthers, John, eds. *Minutes of the Sessions of the Westminster Assembly of Divines, while engaged in preparing their Directory for Church Government, Confession of Faith, and Catechisms* (November 1644 to March 1649). Edinburgh: William Blackwood and Sons, 1874.
   Indispensable for study of the Confession. Introduction is also a useful commentary on the Confession. "Minutes of the Sessions of the Assembly of Divines from August 4, 1643 to April 24, 1652" are also available on microfilm in many libraries.

3. Lightfoot, John. *The Whole Works of the Rev. John Lightfoot, D. D.* Edited by Rev. John Rogers Pitman. Vol. 13. London, 1824.
   This volume contains the *Journal of the Proceedings of the Assembly of Divines: January 1, 1643 to December 31, 1644,* and *Letters to and from Dr. Lightfoot.* This is a record of the Assembly by a participant and covers the period before the Assembly was primarily concerned with the Confession.

4. Baillie, Robert. *The Letters and Journals of Robert Baillie, A.M. Principal of University of Glasgow.* Edited by David Laing. 3 vols. Edinburgh: Robert Ogle, 1841.
   Observations of a Scottish commissioner who had a "nose" for news and gossip.

5. Gillespie, George. "Notes of Debates and Proceedings of the Assembly of Divines and Other Commissioners at Westminster, February 1644 to January 1645" in *The Presbyterian Armory.* Vol. 2. Edinburgh: Robert Ogle and Oliver and Boyd, 1846.

6. *Journals of the House of Commons*

7. *Journals of the House of Lords*

COMMENTARIES ON THE WESTMINSTER CONFESSION

1. Hodge, Archibald Alexander. *A Commentary on the Confession of Faith.* Philadelphia: Presbyterian Board of Christian Education, 1869.

The Confession seen from the perspective of the seventeenth-century theology of Turretin and the development of that theology at Princeton during the nineteenth century.

2. Briggs, Charles Augustus. *Whither, A Theological Question for the Times.* New York: Charles Scribner's Sons, 1889.

   A commentary based on historical study in an effort to determine what the writers of the Confession intended to say, partly in effort to refute the Princeton interpretation.

3. Morris, Edward D. *Theology of the Westminster Symbols, A Commentary Historical, Doctrinal, Practical, on the Confession of Faith and Catechisms and the Related Formularies of the Presbyterian Churches.* Columbus, Ohio, 1900.

   A comprehensive statement of Reformed faith based on the Confession and Catechisms.

4. Dowey, Edward A., Jr. *A Commentary on the Confession of 1967 and An Introduction to the Book of Confessions.* Philadelphia: The Westminster Press, 1968.

   Contains a brief but competent analysis of the Confession.

5. Hendry, George S. *The Westminster Confession for Today; a Contemporary Interpretation.* Richmond: John Knox Press, 1960.

   Useful, but the commentary is more a statement of Christian faith from the Barthian perspective than an effort to understand the Confession.

6. Rogers, Jack Bartlett. *Scripture in the Westminster Confession.* Grand Rapids: William B. Eerdmans Publishing Company, 1967.

   An excellent study of the first chapter of the Confession in the light of writings of those who Roger believes were its authors.

7. Beattie, Francis Robert. *The Presbyterian Standards: An Exposition of the Westminster Confession of Faith and Catechisms.* Richmond: Presbyterian Committee of Publication, 1896.

Histories of the Westminster Assembly

1. Briggs, Charles A. "The Documentary History of Westminster Assembly." *The Presbyterian Review,* I (January 1880): 134 ff.

2. Carruthers, S. W. *The Everyday Work of the Westminster Assembly.* Philadelphia: Presbyterian Historical Society (in America), 1943.

3. Hetherington, W. M. *History of the Westminster Assembly of Divines.* Edited by Robert Williamson. Fifth Edition. New York: Anson D. F. Randolph and Co., 1890.

4. Mitchell, Alexander F. *The Westminster Assembly, Its History and Its Standards*. Philadelphia: Presbyterian Board of Publication, 1884.

5. Mitchell, Alexander F. *Lecture on the Westminster Confession of Faith Being a Contribution to the Study of its Historical Relations and to the Defence of its Teachings*. Edinburgh: Thomas Paton, 1866.

6. Shaw, William A. *A History of the English Church During the Civil Wars and Under the Commonwealth 1640–1660*. Vols. 1–2. London: Longmans, Green, and Co., 1900.

7. Warfield, Benjamin Breckinridge. *The Westminster Assembly and Its Work*. New York: Oxford University Press, 1931.

8. Rogers, Jack Bartlett. *Scripture in the Westminster Confession*. Grand Rapids: William B. Eerdmans Publishing Company, 1967.